Devon &
Cornwall

Walk routes researched and written by David Hancock, Des Hannigan, Brian Pearse and Sue Viccars
Cycle routes researched and written by Sue Viccars
Series managing editor: David Hancock

Produced by AA Publishing
© Automobile Association Developments Limited 2005
First published 2005

Published by AA Publishing (a trading name of Automobile Association Developments Limited, whose registered office is Southwood East, Apollo Rise, Farnborough, Hampshire, GU14 0JW; registered number 1878835).

A02013

Ordnance Survey®   This product includes mapping data licensed from Ordnance Survey® with the permission of the Controller of Her Majesty's Stationery Office. © Crown copyright 2005. All rights reserved. Licence number 399221.

ISBN-10: 0-7495-4449-X
ISBN-13: 978-0-7495-4449-2

A CIP catalogue record for this book is available from the British Library.

The contents of this book are believed correct at the time of printing. Nevertheless, the publishers cannot be held responsible for any errors or omissions or for changes in the details given in this book or for the consequences of any reliance on the information it provides. We have tried to ensure accuracy in this book, but things do change and we would be grateful if readers would advise us of any inaccuracies they may encounter. This does not affect your statutory rights.

We have taken all reasonable steps to ensure that these walks and cycle rides are safe and achievable by people with a realistic level of fitness. However, all outdoor activities involve a degree of risk and the publishers accept no responsibility for any injuries caused to readers whilst following these walks and cycle rides. For advice on walking and cycling in safety, see pages 12 to 15.

Visit AA Publishing's website www.theAA.com/bookshop

Page layouts by pentacorbig, High Wycombe
Colour reproduction by Keene Group, Andover
Printed in Spain by Graficas Estella

AA

Pub Walks &
Cycle Rides
Devon &
Cornwall

Locator map

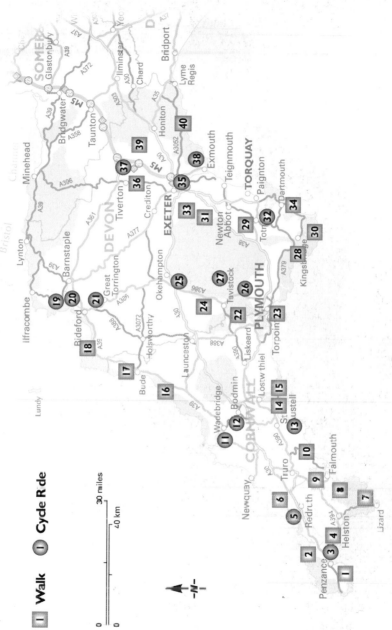

Walk [ ]   **Cyde Rıde** ( )

Contents

Picture on page 4: The rocky River Dart in Dartmoor National Park

Contents

Devon & Cornwall

Well-known as summer holiday destinations, Devon and Cornwall are ideal for walking and cycling. This book includes a range of walk routes, with many circular routes following an outward coastal path and homewards via an inland path. Coastal paths offer uninterrupted views of the sea (and often a surprising number of ups and downs), but also abundant wildlife including seabirds, wildflowers and butterflies. Many cycle routes have been chosen because of the safe, traffic-free nature of the trails. The Camel Trail, the Tarka Trail and the Plym Valley Trail are all off-road routes using trackbeds of former railway lines. Again, there's wildlife to be seen, and pubs along the way positively welcome muddy walkers and cyclists.

Many routes start from or pass through pretty villages, such as Lustleigh, Ashprington and Broadhembury in Devon, and picturesque Cornish fishing villages such as Polruan, across the water from bustling Fowey. You're also never too far from a place to visit if the weather lets you down. Attractions to visit vary from impressive buildings such as Lanhydrock House (National Trust) in the Fowey Valley and Tintagel Castle (English Heritage) with its associations with King Arthur, to the crashing waterfalls at Lydford Gorge and the Bodmin & Wenford Railway. Keen gardeners are really spoilt for choice in Cornwall. The cycle ride from Pentewan has an optional loop to the Lost Gardens of Heligan, and you'll need a full day to see everything that the Eden Project has to offer.

If you prefer a historical element to your day, the Merry Maidens, neolithic standing stones near Lamorna, may appeal. Art-enthusiasts will appreciate the galleries in St Ives and for impressive views, follow the walk which takes you to the top of Brent Tor or admire St Michael's Mount from the walk by Marazion.

Below: The River Fowey in Cornwall

Using this book

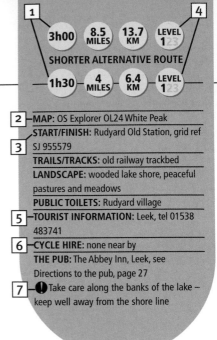

Each walk and cycle ride has a coloured panel giving essential information for the walker and cyclist, including the distance, terrain, nature of the paths, and where to park your car.

1 MINIMUM TIME: The time stated for completing each route is the estimated minimum time that a reasonably fit family group of walkers or cyclists would take to complete the circuit. This does not allow for rest or refreshment stops.

2 MAPS: Each route is shown on a detailed map. However, some detail is lost because of the restrictions imposed by scale, so for this reason, we recommend that you use the maps in conjunction with a more detailed Ordnance Survey map. The relevant Ordnance Survey Explorer map appropriate for each walk or cycle is listed.

3 START/FINISH: Here we indicate the start location and parking area. There is a six-figure grid reference prefixed by two letters showing which 100km square of the National Grid it refers to. You'll find more information on grid references on most Ordnance Survey maps.

4 LEVEL OF DIFFICULTY: The walks and cycle rides have been graded simply (1 to 3) to give an indication of their relative difficulty. Easier routes, such as those with little total ascent, on easy footpaths or level trails, or those covering shorter distances are graded 1. The hardest routes, either because they include a lot of ascent, greater distances, or are in hilly, more demanding terrains, are graded 3.

5 TOURIST INFORMATION: The nearest tourist information office and contact number is given for further local information, in particular opening details for the attractions listed in the 'Where to go from here' section.

6 CYCLE HIRE: We list, within reason, the nearest cycle hire shop/centre.

7 ❶ Here we highlight any potential difficulties or dangers along the route. At a glance you will know if the walk is steep or crosses difficult terrain, or if a cycle route is hilly, encounters a main road, or whether a mountain bike is essential for the off-road trails. If a particular route is suitable for older, fitter children we say so here.

About the pub

Generally, all the pubs featured are on the walk or cycle route. Some are close to the start/finish point, others are at the midway point, and occasionally, the recommended pub is a short drive from the start/finish point. We have included a cross-section of pubs, from homely village locals and isolated rural gems to traditional inns and upmarket country pubs which specialise in food. What they all have in common is that they serve food and welcome children.

The description of the pub is intended to convey its history and character and in the 'food' section we list a selection of dishes, which indicate the style of food available. Under 'family facilities', we say if the pub offers a children's menu or smaller portions of adult dishes, and whether the pub has a family room, highchairs, baby-changing facilities, or toys. There is detail on the garden, terrace, and any play area.

DIRECTIONS: If the pub is very close to the start point we state see Getting to the Start. If the pub is on the route the relevant direction/map location number is given, in addition to general directions. In some cases the pub is a short drive away from the finish point, so we give detailed directions to the pub from the end of the route.

PARKING: The number of parking spaces is given. All but a few of the walks and rides start away from the pub. If the pub car park is the parking/start point, then we have been given permission by the landlord to print the fact. You should always let the landlord or a member of staff know that you are using the car park before setting off.

OPEN: If the pub is open all week we state 'daily' and if it's open throughout the day we say 'all day', otherwise we just give the days/sessions the pub is closed.

FOOD: If the pub serves food all week we state 'daily' and if food is served throughout the day we say 'all day', otherwise we just give the days/sessions when food is not served.

BREWERY/COMPANY: This is the name of the brewery to which the pub is tied or the pub company that owns it. 'Free house' means that the pub is independently owned and run.

REAL ALE: We list the regular real ales available on handpump. 'Guest beers' indicates that the pub rotates beers from a number of microbreweries.

DOGS: We say if dogs are allowed in pubs on walk routes and detail any restrictions.

ROOMS: We list the number of bedrooms and how many are en suite. For prices please call the pub.

Please note that pubs change hands frequently and new chefs are employed, so menu details and facilities may change at short notice. Not all the pubs featured in this guide are listed in the *AA Pub Guide*. For information on those that are, including AA-rated accommodation, and for a comprehensive selection of pubs across Britain, please refer to the *AA Pub Guide* or see the AA's website www.theAA.com

Alternative refreshment stops

At a glance you will see if there are other pubs or cafés along the route. If there are no other places on the route, we list the nearest village or town where you can find somewhere else to eat and drink.

☛ **Where to go from here**

Many of the routes are short and may only take a few hours. You may wish to explore the surrounding area after lunch or before tackling the route, so we have selected a few attractions with children in mind.

Walking and cycling in safety

WALKING

All the walks are suitable for families, but less experienced family groups, especially those with younger children, should try the shorter or easier walks first. Route finding is usually straightforward, but the maps are for guidance only and we recommend that you always take the suggested Ordnance Survey map with you.

Risks

Although each walk has been researched with a view to minimising any risks, no walk in the countryside can be considered to be completely free from risk. Walking in the outdoors will always require a degree of common sense and judgement to ensure that it is as safe as possible, especially for young children.

- Be particularly careful on cliff paths and in upland terrain, where the consequences of a slip can be serious.
- Remember to check tidal conditions before walking on the seashore.
- Some sections of route are by, or cross, busy roads. Remember traffic is a danger even on minor country lanes.
- Be careful around farmyard machinery and livestock.
- Be aware of the consequences of changes in the weather and check the forecast before you set out. Ensure the whole family is properly equipped, wearing warm clothing and a good pair of boots or sturdy walking shoes. Take waterproof clothing with you and carry spare clothing and a torch if you are walking in the winter months. Remember the weather can change quickly at any time of the year, and in moorland and heathland areas, mist and fog can make route finding much harder. In summer, take account of the heat and sun by wearing a hat and carrying enough water.

- On walks away from centres of population you should carry a whistle and survival bag. If you do have an accident requiring emergency services, make a note of your position as accurately as possible and dial 999.

CYCLING

Cycling is a fun activity which children love, and teaching your child to ride a bike, and going on family cycling trips, are rewarding experiences. Not only is cycling a great way to travel, but as a regular form of exercise it can make an invaluable contribution to a child's health and fitness, and increase their confidence and sense of independence.

The growth of motor traffic has made Britain's roads increasingly dangerous and unattractive to cyclists. Cycling with children is an added responsibility and, as with everything, there is a risk when taking them out for a day's cycling. However, in recent years many measures have been taken to address this, including the on-going development of the National Cycle Network (8,000 miles utilising quiet lanes and traffic-free paths) and local designated off-road routes for families, such as converted railway lines, canal towpaths and forest tracks.

In devising the cycle rides in this guide, every effort has been made to use these designated cycle paths, or to link

them with quiet country lanes and waymarked byways and bridleways. Unavoidably, in a few cases, some relatively busy B-roads have been used to link the quieter, more attractive routes.

Rules of the road
- Ride in single file on narrow and busy roads.
- Be alert, look and listen for traffic, especially on narrow lanes and blind bends and be extra careful when descending steep hills, as loose gravel can lead to an accident.
- In wet weather make sure you keep a good distance between you and other riders.
- Make sure you indicate your intentions clearly.
- Brush up on *The Highway Code* before venturing out on to the road.

Off-road safety code of conduct
- Only ride where you know it is legal to do so. It is forbidden to cycle on public footpaths, marked in yellow. The only 'rights of way' open to cyclists are bridleways (blue markers) and unsurfaced tracks, known as byways, which are open to all traffic and waymarked in red.
  - Canal towpaths: you need a permit to cycle on some stretches of towpath (www.waterscape.com). Remember that access paths can be steep and slippery and always get off and push your bike under low bridges and by locks.

- Always yield to walkers and horses, giving adequate warning of your approach.
- Don't expect to cycle at high speeds.
- Keep to the main trail to avoid any unnecessary erosion to the area beside the trail and to prevent skidding, especially if it is wet.
- Remember the Country Code.

Cycling with children

Children can use a child seat from the age of eight months, or from the time they can hold themselves upright. There are a number of child seats available which fit on the front or rear of a bike and towable two-seat trailers are worth investigating. 'Trailer bicycles', suitable for five- to ten-year-olds, can be attached to the rear of an adult's bike, so that the adult has control, allowing the child to pedal if he/she wishes. Family cycling can be made easier by using a tandem, as it can carry a child seat and tow trailers. 'Kiddy-cranks' for shorter legs can be fitted to the rear seat tube, enabling either parent to take their child out cycling. With older children it is better to purchase the right size bike rather than one that is too big, as an oversized bike will be difficult to control, and potentially dangerous.

Preparing your bicycle

A basic routine includes checking the wheels for broken spokes or excess play in the bearings, and checking the tyres for punctures, undue wear and the correct tyre pressures. Ensure that the brake blocks are firmly in place and not worn, and that cables are not frayed or too slack. Lubricate hubs, pedals, gear mechanisms and cables. Make sure you have a pump, a bell, a rear rack to carry panniers and, if cycling at night, a set of working lights.

Preparing yourself

Equipping the family with cycling clothing need not be an expensive exercise. Comfort is the key when considering what to wear. Essential items for well-being on a bike are

padded cycling shorts, warm stretch leggings (avoid tight-fitting and seamed trousers like jeans or baggy tracksuit trousers that may become caught in the chain), stiff-soled training shoes, and a wind and waterproof jacket. Fingerless gloves will add to your comfort.

A cycling helmet provides essential protection if you fall off your bike, so they are particularly recommended for young children learning to cycle.

Wrap your child up with several layers in colder weather. Make sure you and those with you are easily visible by car drivers and other road users, by wearing light-coloured or luminous clothing in daylight and reflective strips or sashes in failing light and when it is dark.

What to take with you

Invest in a pair of medium-sized panniers (rucksacks are unwieldy and can affect balance) to carry the necessary gear for you and your family for the day. Take extra clothes with you, the amount depending on the season, and always pack a light wind/waterproof jacket. Carry a basic tool kit (tyre levers, adjustable spanner, a small screwdriver, puncture repair kit, a set of Allen keys) and practical spares, such as an inner tube, a universal brake/gear cable, and a selection of nuts and bolts. Also, always take a pump and a strong lock.

Cycling, especially in hilly terrain and off-road, saps energy, so take enough food and drink for your outing. Always carry plenty of water, especially in hot and humid weather conditions. Consume high-energy snacks like cereal bars, cake or fruits, eating little and often to combat feeling weak and tired. Remember that children get thirsty (and hungry) much more quickly than adults so always have food and diluted juices available for them.

And finally, the most important advice of all—enjoy yourselves!

NATIONAL CYCLE NETWORK

A comprehensive network of safe and attractive cycle routes throughout the UK.

It is co-ordinated by the route construction charity Sustrans with the support of more than 450 local authorities and partners across Britain. For maps, leaflets and more information on the designated off-road cycle trails across the country contact
www.sustrans.org.uk
www.nationalcyclenetwork.org.uk

LONDON CYCLING CAMPAIGN

Pressure group that lobbies MPs, organises campaigns and petitions in order to improve cycling conditions in the capital. It provides maps, leaflets and information on cycle routes across London.
www.lcc.org.uk

BRITISH WATERWAYS

For information on towpath cycling, visit
www.waterscape.com

FORESTRY COMMISSION

For information on cycling in Forestry Commission woodland see
www.forestry.gov.uk/recreation

CYCLISTS TOURING CLUB

The largest cycling club in Britain, provides information on cycle touring, and legal and technical matters
www.ctc.org.uk

A circular walk to Lamorna

Lamorna · CORNWALL

A coastal and inland walk from Lamorna Cove, passing an ancient stone circle.

Quarries and standing stones

The walk starts from popular, picturesque Lamorna Cove, once the scene of granite quarrying. The quay at Lamorna was built so that ships could load up with the quarried stone, but the tidal regimen made berthing difficult. Much of the stone was carried overland.

The coast path west from Lamorna winds its sinuous way through tumbled granite boulders, then climbs steeply to the cliff tops. Soon the path descends steeply to the delightful St Loy's Cove, a secluded boulder beach. Spring comes early at St Loy; the subtropical vegetation through which the walk leads reflects the area's mild and moist micro-climate. From St Loy's woods you climb inland to reach two enthralling monuments. The first is the Tregiffian burial chamber, a late Bronze Age entrance grave.

Just along the road from Tregiffian is the Merry Maidens stone circle. This late Neolithic/Bronze Age structure is an ancient ceremonial and ritual site of major importance. The final part of the walk leads to a wonderful old trackway that leads over water-worn stones into the Lamorna Valley along a route that may well have originated in the time of the stone circles themselves.

the walk

1 From the far end of the seaward car park in the cove, at the end of the terrace above **Lamorna Harbour**, follow the coast path through some short rocky sections. Continue along the coast path past the tops of Tregurnow Cliff and Rosemodress Cliff.

The Merry Maidens. Legend has it that 19 young girls were turned to stone here

3h30 · **6 MILES** · **9.7 KM** · **LEVEL 123**

2 Pass the **nature reserve** (open access) set up by author Derek Tangye, who lived along this coast, then pass above the entrance ramp and steps to **Tater du Lighthouse**. Pass a large residence on the right and then, where the track bends right, keep left along the narrow coast path, at a signpost.

3 Descend steeply (take great care when the ground is muddy) from Boscawen Cliff to **St Loy's Cove**. Cross a section of sea-smoothed boulders that may be slippery when wet. Follow the path inland through dense vegetation and by the stream. Cross a private drive then climb steeply uphill. Go over a stile onto a track, turn right over a stile and follow the path through trees.

4 By a **wooden signpost** and three trees, go sharply down right and cross the stream on large boulders, then follow a hedged-in path round left. In about 50yds (46m), by a wooden signpost, go sharp right and up to a surfaced lane. Turn left and follow the lane uphill. At a junction with a bend on another track, keep ahead and uphill. At **Boskenna Farm** buildings follow the surfaced lane round left and keep ahead.

5 From the lane, at the entrance drive to a bungalow on the right, the right-of-way goes through a field gate (not signed), then cuts across the field corner to a wooden stile in a wire fence. Beyond this, the way (there's no path) leads diagonally across the field to its top right-hand corner, where a stile leads into a large roadside lay-by with a **granite cross** at its edge.

A striking variety of rocks around the shore at Lamorna Cove

MAP: OS Explorer 102 Land's End
START/FINISH: Lamorna Cove; parking at the Quay; grid ref: SW 450241
PATHS: good coastal footpaths, field paths and rocky tracks
LANDSCAPE: picturesque coastline, fields and wooded valleys, 7 stiles
PUBLIC TOILETS: Lamorna Cove
TOURIST INFORMATION: Penzance, tel 01736 362207
THE PUB: Lamorna Wink, Lamorna
🛈 Undulating, rugged and stony coast path; a few steep ascents and descents; suitable for older, more experienced children

Getting to the start
Lamorna Cove is signposted off the B3315 between Penzance and Land's End, 4 miles (6.4km) west of Penzance via Newlyn. Drive through Lamorna village, passing the Lamorna Wink to the cove and parking area.

Researched and written by:
David Hancock, Des Hannigan

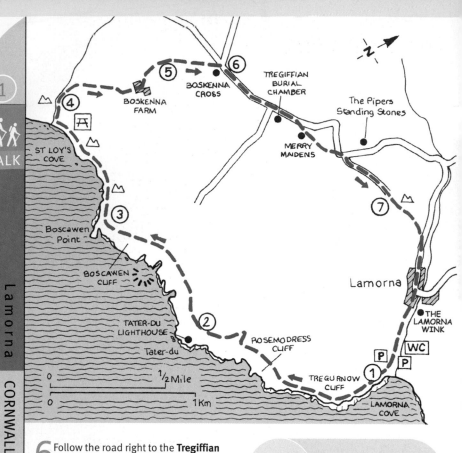

6 Follow the road right to the **Tregiffian burial chamber** on the right and then to the **Merry Maidens stone circle**. From the stone circle continue to a field corner, then cross over a steep wall stile by a gate. Follow a path diagonally right across the next field towards buildings. Go over a stone stile onto a road, then go down the left-hand of two lanes, a surfaced lane with a 'No Through Road' sign.

7 Where the lane ends keep ahead onto a **public bridleway**. Follow a shady and very rocky track downhill to the public road. Turn right and walk down the road, with care, passing the **Lamorna Wink pub**, to the car park.

what to look for

If you do this walk in spring you will be treated to a genuine 'host of golden daffodils'. The cliffside paths are flanked by hundreds of daffodils that have spread from cultivated meadows. Until recent years, flower-growing was an important element in the small-scale market gardening carried out along this western coast of Mount's Bay. Another marvellous floral display is offered by the swathes of bluebells, found on the open cliffs and in the lush woodland behind St Loy's Cove.

Lamorna Wink

This oddly named pub was one of the original Kiddleywinks, a product of the 1830 Beer Act that enabled any householder to buy a liquor licence. Popular with walkers and tourists exploring the rugged Penwith Peninsula, the Wink is an unspoilt, no-frills country local decorated with warship mementoes, sea photographs and nautical brassware. One of the simply furnished rooms has a pool table and books for sale, while the homely main bar is warmed in winter by a glowing coal fire. You'll find tip-top Cornish beer on tap, best enjoyed in summer at one of the picnic benches to the front or in the side garden.

Food

Expect a limited lunchtime menu offering sandwiches, filled jacket potatoes, fresh local crab, salads and ploughman's lunches.

Family facilities

Children are welcome in the eating areas of the bar

Alternative refreshment stops

There is a shop and a café at Lamorna Cove by the car park.

☛ Where to go from here

Combine a visit to one of Cornwall's finest beaches at Porthcurno with a tour of the Museum of Submarine Telegraphy, housed in underground tunnels that were the centre of the British communications system during World War Two (www.porthcurno.org.uk). Don't miss the Minack Theatre built high on the cliffs above Porthcurno by one remarkable woman: Rowena Cade. There are few better backdrops for plays than the one at this famous little theatre – dramatic cliffs and blue sea stretching into the distance. Time your visit to one of the summer season plays (www.minack.com).

about the pub

Lamorna Wink
Lamorna, Penzance
Cornwall TR19 6XH
Tel 01736 731566

DIRECTIONS: see Getting to the start	
PARKING: 40	
OPEN: daily; all day in summer	
FOOD: lunchtimes only (check in winter)	
BREWERY/COMPANY: free house	
REAL ALE: Sharp's Doom Bar, Skinner's Cornish Knocker	
DOGS: allowed inside	

A coastal walk near St Ives

A short walk through St Ives and along the rocky coast, returning along old paths.

St Ives coast path

In the days before better transport, the scenic road from St Ives to St Just, along the north coast of the Land's End peninsula, was no more than a rough track used for carrying heavier loads by cart and wagon. Even before this track evolved people travelled more easily on foot along the coastal belt below the hills. Until the early 20th century the field paths, with their granite stiles, were used by local people.

The coastal paths on the outer edge of this wonderful mosaic of ancient fields barely existed in earlier times. They were useful only to individual farms directly inland and were often mere links between paths down to isolated coves. As commerce and foreign wars increased, the coastline of South West England came under much closer scrutiny by the authorities. When 19th-century smuggling was at its height, government 'revenue men' patrolled here. In later years the coastguard service also patrolled the coast on foot until most sections were passable, by footpath at least. Linking these paths created today's coastal footpath.

This walk starts from the heart of St Ives and heads west for a short distance along the glorious coastline. This is a very remote and wild part of the West Cornwall coast, a landscape of exquisite colours in spring and summer. The route turns inland and plunges into a lush, green countryside that seems, at times, far removed from the sea. Field paths lead unswervingly back towards St Ives with a sequence of granite stiles reminding you that this journey was an everyday event for Cornish folk.

(**1h45**) (**3.25** MILES) (**5.2** KM) (**LEVEL** 1 2 3)

(2)

WALK

St Ives | CORNWALL

the walk

1 Walk along the harbour front towards Smeaton's Pier. Just before the pier entrance, turn left up **Sea View Place**. Where the road bends, keep straight on into Wheal Dream. Turn right past **St Ives Museum**, then follow a walkway to **Porthgwidden Beach**.

2 Cross the car park above the beach and climb to the **National Coastwatch lookout**. Climb to the chapel on the headland via a path behind the lookout, then follow a footway down to **Porthmeor Beach**. Go along the beach up to the car park.

3 Go up steps beside the public toilets, then turn right along a surfaced track past bowling and putting greens. Continue to the rocky headlands of **Carrick Du** and **Clodgy Point**.

4 From the distinctive square-cut rock on Clodgy Point walk uphill and through a low wall. Follow the path round to the right and across a wet area. In about 0.5 mile (800m) go left at a junction.

5 Reach a T-junction with a track just past a National Trust sign, **'Hellesveor Cliff'**. Turn left and head inland, following a hedged-in track, which is probably centuries-old. Such tracks gave access to the cliff, where animals were grazed and where the stone was gathered for building and furze for fuel. Go through a gate, continue up the hedged track and cross the stone stile in the hedge on your left where the track curves sharp left.

MAP: OS Explorer 102 Land's End
START/FINISH: Upper Trenwith car park St Ives or Porthmeor Beach, grid ref: SW 522408
PATHS: promenade, coastal path (can be quite rocky), field paths, 6 stiles
LANDSCAPE: town, scenic coast and small inland fields
PUBLIC TOILETS: Smeaton's Pier and Porthmeor car park
TOURIST INFORMATION: St Ives, tel 01736 796297
THE PUB: The Sloop Inn, St Ives
The coast path can be rocky and wet in places; busy town streets

Getting to the start
St Ives is on the A3074, 4 miles (6.4km) north of the A30 between Penzance and Camborne. Follow signs for the main town (Upper Trenwith), or follow signs through the town centre, or off the B3306 west of the town centre, to the Tate Gallery, to locate the car park at Porthmeor Beach.

Researched and written by: David Hancock, Des Hannigan

6 Follow the path through the field and across a stile. Go through a metal gate, pass a field gap and down a hedged-in path. Cross a stile and pass between high hedges to reach a lane

7 Turn right along the lane (**Burthallan Lane**) to a T-junction with the main road. Turn left and follow the road downhill to Porthmeor Beach and the car park.

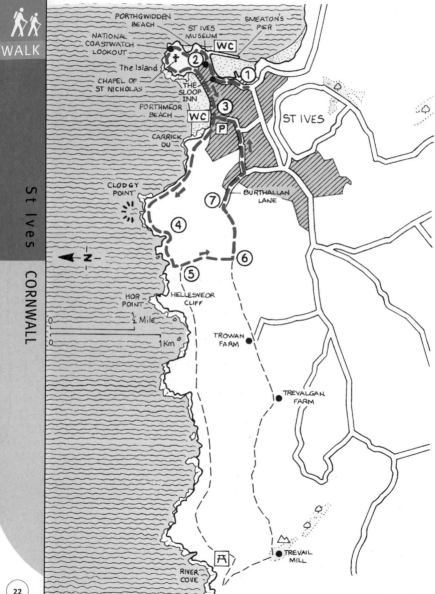

The Sloop Inn

Close to 700 years old, the famous Sloop is one of Cornwall's oldest inns. Only a cobbled courtyard and a road separate it from the harbour, making it handy, not just for fisherman, but for locals, some of them painters, and families spending the day on the beach. Paintings by artists associated with the St Ives School hang in the panelled cellar and low-beamed lounge bars. The flagstoned public bar, with its unusual long tables, has frequently appeared on TV and in films. Arrive early to bag an outside table with its bustling harbour views. The pub is well placed for the Tate Gallery and the Barbara Hepworth Museum.

Food

The speciality is locally caught fresh fish and shellfish, so mackerel, mussels, smoked haddock fishcakes, seafood chowder, monkfish and prawn casserole, and cod in beer batter are likely to be on the menu. Alternatives include filled baguettes, pasta meals, home-made lamb and mint pie, and bangers and mash.

Family facilities

Children are welcome in the eating areas.

Alternative refreshment stops

You are spoilt for choice for pubs, cafés and restaurants in St Ives.

☛ Where to go from here

At the start of the walk the St Ives Museum is a delightfully venerable institution portraying the history and culture of St Ives with some panache. Above Porthmeor Beach is the splendid Tate Gallery St Ives (www.tate.org.uk), a custom-built gallery celebrating the work of the mainly Modernist St Ives painters. Take a drive south west along the dramatic Penwith coast, via the interesting Wayside Folk Museum at Zennor, to the Geevor Tin Mine Heritage Centre at Pendeen. Explore the surface buildings of the mine, see the fascinating museum and follow the expert guide into Wheal Mexico, where Cornish miners worked over 200 years ago (www.geevor.com).

about the pub

The Sloop Inn

The Wharf, St Ives
Cornwall TR26 1LP
Tel 01736 796584
www.sloop-inn.co.uk

DIRECTIONS: see Getting to the start; pub overlooks harbour between Points **1** and **2**
PARKING: use town car parks
OPEN: daily; all day
FOOD: daily
BREWERY/COMPANY: Unique
REAL ALE: John Smith's Bitter, Sharp's Doom Bar, Greene King Old Speckled Hen, Bass
DOGS: allowed inside
ROOMS: 16 bedrooms, 13 en suite

Marazion to Penzance

CYCLE

Marazion   CORNWALL

Enjoy an easy ride along one of south Cornwall's most beautiful bays.

St Michael's Mount

Marazion – and the whole of Mount's Bay – is dominated by the rocky bulk of St Michael's Mount, accessible by foot via the 600yd (549m) causeway at low tide, and by ferry from the beach when the tide is up (weather permitting). This extraordinary granite outcrop is topped by a medieval castle, dating from the 12th century and now mainly in the care of the National Trust. Originally the site of a Benedictine priory, it has been the home of the St Aubyn family for over 300 years. There is also a 14th-century church on the rock, as well as a pub, restaurant and shops round the little harbour, and a private garden with limited opening times. Marazion Marsh, passed on the right of the road near the start of the ride, is the largest reedbed in Cornwall. An RSPB nature reserve, this area of reedbeds, open water and willow carr attracts overwintering bitterns, sedge, Cetti's and reed warblers, butterflies and damselflies. There is a hide from which the birds can be watched (including the rare, spotted crake) and good access via boardwalks.

the ride

1 This ride is part of the First and Last Trail, the first stretch of the Cornish Way long-distance cycle route, which starts at Land's End and runs for 180 miles (288km) through the county. Marazion, where this ride starts, is Cornwall's oldest charter town, dating from 1257. Its unusual name comes from the Cornish 'marghas yow' – Thursday market. Marazion was the main trading port in Mount's Bay until Penzance overtook it in the 16th century. It's worth having a look around this attractive village before you set off.

From the pub car park cycle uphill (away from the beach) onto West End. (The Godolphin Arms can be found by turning right.) Turn left along **West End** and cycle out of the village. There is a parking area on the left along much of this road, so look out for people opening their car doors suddenly. **Marazion Marsh** lies to the right.

2 Where the road bears right to cross the Penzance to Exeter main railway line, keep straight ahead through a **parking area**, with the Pizza Shack (and toilets behind) on the right. Again, take care cycling through the car park.

St Michael's Mount seen from across the river

| 1h30 | 5 MILES | 8 KM | LEVEL 1 2 3 |

MAP: OS Explorer 102 Land's End
START/FINISH: The Godolphin Arms car park, Marazion, grid ref: SW 516306
TRAILS/TRACKS: short stretch of road, track generally level, rough and bumpy in places
LANDSCAPE: village, beach, seaside, townscape
PUBLIC TOILETS: on Points **2** and **3** of the route, and in the car park at Penzance
TOURIST INFORMATION: Penzance, tel 01736 362207
CYCLE HIRE: The Cycle Centre, Penzance, tel 01736 351671
THE PUB: The Godolphin Arms, Marazion
🅛 Short stretch of road at start and finish, one car park to be negotiated

Getting to the start
From Penzance, take the A30 past the heliport. At the second roundabout turn right, signed Marazion. The Godolphin Arms car park is signed right (towards the beach).

Why do this cycle ride?
This level, easy, there-and-back route along the edge of Mount's Bay, with spectacular views over St Michael's Mount, is an ideal option for families with young children. With just a short road stretch at the start and finish, the ride runs along the back of the huge expanse of sands between Marazion and Penzance, originally a tiny fishing community, today popular with tourists.

Researched and written by: Sue Viccars

3 Keep ahead and leave the car park to the left of the old station (now the **Station pub**), to join a level track that runs along the back of the beach. Follow this track, passing more public toilets on the right.

St Michael's Mount, seen from Marazion

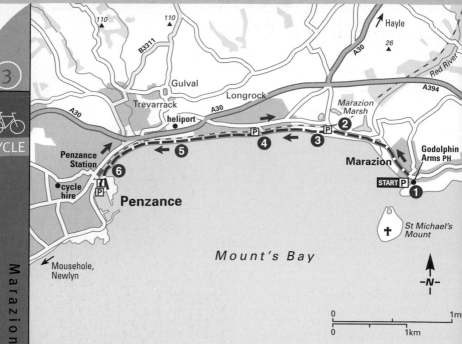

4 Take care where the track drops to meet an entrance road to a **beachside car park** (there are warning notices 'Give way to traffic'). Pass through the parking area and continue along the track, with the railway close by on the right.

5 Pass the **heliport**, from which helicopters fly regularly to the Isles of Scilly, which lie more than 17 miles (28 km) southwest of Land's End (day trips are available). Good views open up ahead towards Penzance.

6 On approaching the station the track narrows into a concrete walkway and becomes busier, so look out for pedestrians. Follow the track into the car park by Penzance railway and bus station, with the **tourist information centre** to the right. This is where you should turn round and return to Marazion. The First and Last

Trail actually runs along the road to Newlyn and beyond, but is pretty busy in terms of traffic and is not recommended for families with young children.

There is a lot to see in Penzance, however, which developed as in important pilchard fishing centre in medieval times. Penzance, Newlyn and Mousehole (along the coast to the west) were all destroyed by Spanish raiders in 1595, but by the early 17th century Penzance's fortunes had revived on account of the export of tin from local mines, and it became a fashionable place to live. The coming of the Great Western Railway in Victorian times gave the town another boost and it is now the main centre in Penwith (the far western part of Cornwall). The harbour is always full of interest, and it is from here that the RMV *Scillonian* makes regular sailings to the Isles of Scilly.

The Godolphin Arms

Located right at the water's edge opposite St Michael's Mount, The Godolphin Arms affords superb views across the bay. It's so close that the sea splashes at the windows in the winter and you can watch the movement of seals, dolphins, ferries and fishing boats. From the traditional wood-floored bar and beer terrace to the light and airy restaurant and most of the bedrooms, the Mount is clearly visible.

Food

The bar menu offers a choice of salads, sandwiches, light bites such as pan-fried sardines and spicy meatballs, and seafood tagliatelle, or ham, egg and chips. Seafood features prominently on the dinner menu, perhaps line-caught whole sea bass stuffed with thyme and lemon.

Family facilities

Children of all ages are allowed in the pub. There's an area set aside for families, and high chairs and baby-changing facilities for young children. Smaller portions from the main menu, a children's menu and two family bedrooms are also available. The beach is just below the pub's rear terrace.

about the pub

The Godolphin Arms
West End, Marazion
Penzance, Cornwall TR17 0EN
Tel 01736 710202
www.godolphinarms.co.uk

DIRECTIONS: see Getting to the start	
PARKING: 70	
OPEN: daily; all day	
FOOD: daily; all day in summer	
BREWERY/COMPANY: free house	
REAL ALE: Sharp's Special and Eden Ale, Skinner's Spriggan	
ROOMS: 10 en suite	

Alternative refreshment stops

There are plenty of pubs, cafés and restaurants in both Marazion and Penzance.

☛ Where to go from here

Head for Newlyn where you will find Britain's only working salt pilchard factory, the Pilchard Works, where you can experience at first hand a Cornish factory that has continued producing salt pilchards for over 90 years (www.pilchardworks.co.uk). Art lovers should visit the Penlee House Gallery and Museum in Penzance (www.penleehouse.org.uk) to learn more about the Newlyn School of Artists and view one of the regular exhibitions. Kids will enjoy a visit to the Lighthouse Centre in Penzance or to the Wild Bird Hospital and Sanctuary in Mousehole. For information about St Michael's Mount see www.nationaltrust.org.uk.

Prussia Cove coastal walk

A stroll through the coastal domain of one of Cornwall's most famous smugglers.

Prussia Cove

Smuggling clings to the image of Cornwall: old time 'freetraders' stole ashore with their cargoes of tea, spirits, tobacco and silk. Modern smuggling, chiefly of drugs, has no such romantic sheen yet we attach an image of honest adventure to old-time smuggling.

Such 'honest adventuring' seems personified by the famous Carter family which lived at Prussia Cove. The cove is really more of a series of rocky inlets close

to the magnificent St Michael's Mount, the castle-crowned island that so enhances the inner corner of Mount's Bay. John and Henry (Harry) Carter were the best known members of the family and ran their late 18th-century smuggling enterprise with great flair and efficiency. John Carter was the more flamboyant, styling himself in early childhood games as 'the King of Prussia'. The name stuck and the original Porth Leah Cove became known as the 'King of Prussia's Cove'. Fame indeed. John Carter had integrity. He once broke in to an excise store in Penzance to recover smuggled goods confiscated from Prussia Cove in his absence. The authorities knew it must

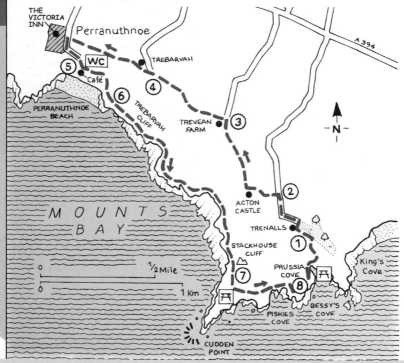

have been Carter because he was 'an upright man' and took only his own goods. His brother Harry became a Methodist preacher and forbade swearing on all his vessels.

As you follow this walk inland, you sense the remoteness of hamlets, the secretiveness of the lanes and paths. At Perranuthnoe, the beach resounds with the sound of the sea where surfers and holidaymakers now enjoy themselves. From here the coastal footpath leads back across the rocky headland of Cudden Point.

the walk

1 From the car park entrance walk back along the approach road, past the large house. Watch for traffic. After the second bend, look for a **stile** on the left, just past a field gate.

2 Cross the stile and follow the left-hand field edge, bearing off to the right, where it bends left, to reach a stile in the hedge opposite. Walk down the edge of the next field, behind Acton Castle (private dwellings), then turn right along field edges to a stile into the adjacent **rough lane**. Turn right.

3 Pass a house called **Acton Barns** and turn left along a rough track at a junction in front of a bungalow entrance at **Trevean Farm**. At a left-hand bend go onto a stony track for just a few paces, then look out for the **public footpath sign**, ascend to the right, up some narrow steps, then turn left along the edge of the field.

Prussia Cove, once the haunt of smugglers

2h00 — 4 MILES — 6.4 KM — LEVEL 1 2 3

MAP: OS Explorer 102 Land's End

START/FINISH: Trenalls, Prussia Cove. Small, privately-owned car park; grid ref: SW 554283. Alternatively, park at Perranuthnoe, from where the walk can be started at Point **5**

PATHS: good field paths and coastal paths, 18 stiles

LANDSCAPE: quiet coast and countryside

PUBLIC TOILETS: Perranuthnoe

TOURIST INFORMATION: Penzance, tel 01736 362207

THE PUB: Victoria Inn, Perranuthnoe

🛈 Care to be taken on the cliff path near Prussia Cove

Getting to the start

Prussia Cove is signposted off the A394 at Rosudgeon between Penzance and Helston, 6 miles (9.7km) east of Penzance. Follow the narrow lane to its end at Trenalls. The parking area is just past the farm at the end of the tarmac road.

Researched and written by: David Hancock, Des Hannigan

7 At the National Trust property of **Cudden Point,** follow the path steeply uphill and then across the inner slope of the headland above **Piskies Cove**.

8 Go through a gate and pass some ancient fishing huts. Follow the path round the edge of the **Bessy's Cove** inlet of Prussia Cove, to reach a track by a thatched cottage. The cove can be reached down a path on the right just before this junction. Turn right and follow the track. Ignore the track left by the postbox and take the second left (**green sign**) to return to the car park at the start of the walk.

The beach at Perranuthnoe

4 At Trebarvah, cross the farm lane, pass in front of some barns, (there's a view of St Michael's Mount ahead), then follow the right-hand field edge to a hedged-in path. Follow the path ahead through fields, then pass in front of some houses to reach the main road opposite the **Victoria Inn**. Go left and follow the road to the car park above **Perranuthnoe Beach**.

5 For the beach and Cabin Café keep straight ahead. On the main route of the walk, go left, just beyond the car park, and along a lane. Bear right at a fork, then bear right again just past a house at a junction.

6 Go down a track towards the sea and follow it round left. Then, at a field entrance, go down right (signposted), turn sharp left through a gap and follow the **coast path** along the edge of Trebarvah and **Stackhouse Cliffs**.

what to look for

Along the sandy paths and fields east of Perranuthnoe, the feathery-leafed tamaraisk (Tamarix anglica), lends an exotic Mediterranean atmosphere to the Cornish scene. The tamarisk was introduced to Britain from the Mediterranean and is often used at coastal locations as a windbreak because of its resilience and its ability to survive the battering of salt-laden winds. Take time midway in the walk to enjoy Perranuthnoe Beach, known as Perran Sands, a fine little beach, which is south-facing and catches the sun all day. It's also worth exploring Prussia Cove itself and its individual rocky inlets. This is a good place for a swim at low tide in the crystal clear water.

Victoria Inn

Situated on a peaceful lane leading up to the parish church, this 12th-century inn was built to accommodate the masons constructing the church and is reputed to be one of the oldest in Cornwall. The pretty, pink-washed exterior is adorned with hanging baskets and the inn sign shows a very young Queen Victoria. Inside, the large, L-shaped bar has a beamed ceiling, some exposed stone walls, an open log fire, and a snug alcove for intimate dining. Local coastal and wreck photographs and various maritime memorabilia decorate the bar. In summer you can sit outside in the sheltered, Mediterranean-style patio garden.

Food
Expect daily fresh fish and seafood like Dover sole, scallops and crevettes in garlic and monkfish with basil sauce, as well as wild boar steak with cider sauce, slow roasted lamb, and lunchtime snacks – baguettes, ploughman's and filled jacket potatoes.

Family facilities
Young children are welcome in the dining areas. There are high chairs available as well as a children's menu and smaller portions of adult dishes.

Alternative refreshment stops
On the approach to Perranuthnoe Beach is the busy little Cabin Café, open all summer and at weekends in winter.

☛ Where to go from here
Reached on foot by a causeway at low tide, or by ferry at high tide in the summer only, St Michael's Mount rises dramatically from the sea, with its medieval castle, to which a magnificent east wing was added in the 1870s (www.nationaltrust.org.uk). Nearby Godolphin House at Godolphin Cross is a romantic Tudor and Stuart mansion that is being beautifully restored by English Heritage (www.goldolphinhouse.com). Children will enjoy visiting the Paradise Park Wildlife Sanctuary at Hayle, where they can see rare and beautiful tropical birds, otters and red squirrels, and explore the Fun Farm and play areas (www.paradisepark.org.uk).

about the pub

Victoria Inn
Perranuthnoe, Penzance
Cornwall TR20 9NP
Tel 01736 710309
www.victoriainn-penzance.co.uk

DIRECTIONS: village signposted off the A394 0.5 mile (800m) east of the junction with the B3280. Point **4** on the walk

PARKING: 10

OPEN: daily

FOOD: daily

BREWERY/COMPANY: Innspired

REAL ALE: Bass, Sharp's Doom Bar, Greene King Abbot Ale

DOGS: allowed in the bar

ROOMS: 3 en suite

Portreath tramroad

A fascinating exploration of Cornwall's industrial past.

Mining memorabilia

This ride is just bursting with industrial and natural history. The Portreath Tramroad (along which wagons were originally drawn by horses) was the first of its kind in Cornwall, and the section to Scorrier was active from 1812 until the mid 1860s, linking important tin- and copper-mining areas with the harbour at Portreath. The Wheal Busy Loop, positively stuffed with old engine houses, gives an indication of how much industrial activity went on in this now somewhat bleak area in the 18th and 19th centuries. One of the first Newcomen steam engines was built here in 1725, and later Wheal Busy boasted the first James Watt steam engine in Cornwall. Nearby Chacewater was once a prosperous mining village, as evidenced by the number of fine Georgian and Victorian shop fronts preserved today.

Unity Wood is full of old shafts and workings too, and mining for tin here dates from opencast methods (known as 'coffinworks') in medieval times. Today these tranquil remains provide suitable conditions for a good range of flora and fauna: the common blue and green hairstreak butterfly, pipistrelles and greater horseshoe bats (roosting in the deserted mine shafts), and dragonflies and damselflies dancing above the old mine ponds.

the ride

1 From the car park turn left and follow it inland past the **Portreath Arms Hotel** (left). Just past the hotel bear left along narrow Sunny Vale Road. Where this bears

right to rejoin the B3300 bear left onto the **tramway**. Follow this through woodland and over the access road to a reservoir. Continue through woodland, then fields, eventually reaching a drive with a white cottage on the left. Keep ahead along a narrow lane to reach a minor road. Drop down to cross the road at **Cambrose**.

2 Turn left and cycle along the pavement (cycle lane), following the road past **Elm Farm** (left). Around 500yds (457m) later, where the road bears left, turn right on a quiet lane to a T-junction at **Lower Forge**. Cross the road and keep ahead along a lane. Keep ahead at the next T-junction onto the tramway again. Follow this to its end at North Downs (1.75 miles/2.8km); turn left to meet a road. Turn right along the pavement (cycle lane) to the roundabout.

(For the Fox and Hounds pub – and so **the shorter route** – keep ahead round the right edge of the roundabout to cross the A30. Follow the pavement round to the right and cross the road by the Crossroads Motel. Follow the road under the railway bridge and bear left; the pub will be found on the right.)

3 For the **Wheal Busy Loop** – which is quite hard, but highly recommended – turn left across the road and follow the pavement, keeping the roundabout right. Keep uphill past another small roundabout, then Smokey Joe's café on the left. At the top of the hill turn right to cross the **A30**.

4 Just over the bridge turn left down a rough track. Bear left at **Boscawen Farm** and follow the track as it undulates past the remains of Boscawen Mine. Pass **Wheal Busy chapel** left, to reach a lane junction. Keep ahead; 109 yards (100m) on turn right down a rough bridleway. Turn right on a track at the bottom. Drop gently downhill, passing to the left of **old mine buildings** at Wheal Busy. Keep ahead and cross a small lane, then head steadily uphill, bearing left at the top to meet a road.

5 Cross over and follow a track through a small parking area and downhill past Killifreth Mine's **Hawke's Shaft pumping house** (with the tallest chimney stack in Cornwall, and shafts up to 600ft/183m deep). Enter **Unity Woods**; keep left at the fork and follow the bumpy track downhill to a junction.

6 Turn right, rejoining the **tramway**. Follow the track out of the woods, with fields right and a road (B3298) left. Cross the road where signed – take care – and continue along the track to the left of the road. At the junction turn left to push along the pavement. After 109 yards (100m) turn right to cross the road, passing to the right of the Fox and Hounds pub. At the next road turn left and pass under the railway bridge. At the T-junction by the **Crossroads Motel**, cross over and turn right on the pavement to cross the A30 and rejoin the outward route.

3h00 · **13.5 MILES** · **21.7 KM** · **LEVEL 2**

SHORTER ALTERNATIVE ROUTE

2h00 · **10 MILES** · **16 KM** · **LEVEL 2**

MAP: OS Explorer 104 Redruth & St Agnes

START/FINISH: beach car park in Portreath, grid ref: SW 654453

TRAILS/TRACKS: mainly well-surfaced track, extension rough and rocky, some roadwork

LANDSCAPE: woodland and fields, heath, old mine workings

PUBLIC TOILETS: none on route

TOURIST INFORMATION: Helston, tel 01326 565431

CYCLE HIRE: Elm Farm, on the tramroad near Portreath, tel 01209 891498

THE PUB: Bassett Arms, Portreath

🚴 Busy roads with good, marked pavements and some rough sections on the Wheal Busy Loop

Getting to the start

Portreath is about 4 miles (6.4km) north west of Redruth, and is signed off the A30 on the B3300. Park in the car park by the beach.

Why do this cycle ride?

The Coast-to-Coast Trail follows the Portreath Tramroad as far as Scorrier. This ride takes you into the heart of old industrial Cornwall, following a trail that runs across the county for 11 miles (17.5km) to Devoran on Restronguet Creek. The optional Wheal Busy Loop, explores an area peppered with old engine houses.

Researched and written by: Sue Viccars

Portreath CORNWALL

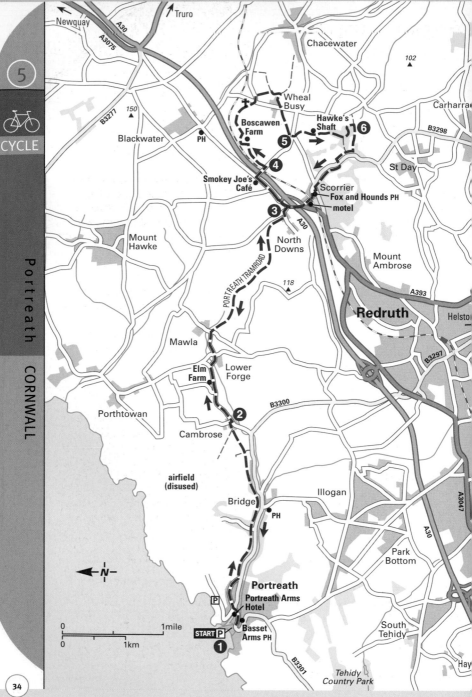

Bassett Arms

The Bassett Arms is a typical Cornish cottage, built as a pub in the early 19th century to serve the harbour workers, with plenty of tin mining and shipwreck memorabilia adorning the low-beamed interior. Today, it serves the many cyclists using the mineral tramways cycle path to Devoran – the pub is conveniently located at the start point – and the beach is just a short stroll away. There are cycle racks in the car park and a sunny terrace and garden for summer days. In winter, there's a comfortable bar with an open fire and a big conservatory dining room to relax in after the ride.

Food

Bar food is hearty and traditional, ranging from bacon sandwiches, filled jacket potatoes and seaside salads (prawn or Cornish yarg), to grills with all the trimmings and daily specials like steak and ale pie and fresh local fish. Good value Sunday roast lunches and summer weekend barbecues in the garden.

Family facilities

Children are welcome throughout the pub and youngsters have a standard children's menu to choose from. There is also an adventure play area in the garden.

Alternative refreshment stops

There's at least one beach café and the Portreath Arms Hotel in Portreath, while on route you'll find the Fox and Hounds pub on the shorter loop.

☛ Where to go from here

At Pool near Redruth you can see impressive relics of the tin mining industry at the Cornish Mines and Engines, namely great beam engines and a fascinating industrial heritage centre in a converted mine. Informative guided tours take you through the ancient process of cider making at the Cornish Cyder Farm at Penhallow (www.thecornishcyderfarm.co.uk). Head for Truro and spend some time at the Royal Cornwall Museum and learn more about the county in well laid-out galleries displaying artefacts from the stone age, Cornish wildlife and 21st-century studio pottery (www.royalcornwallmuseum.org.uk).

about the pub

Bassett Arms
Tregea Terrace, Portreath
Redruth, Cornwall TR16 4NG
Tel 01209 842077
www.ccinns.co.uk

DIRECTIONS: from the beach car park turn right and follow the road round to the left to the pub

PARKING: 25

OPEN: daily; all day Saturday and Sunday and July to September

FOOD: daily

BREWERY/COMPANY: Coast and Country Inns

REAL ALE: Sharp's Doom Bar, Wadworth 6X, Greene King Abbot Ale

St Agnes Head to St Agnes Beacon

A bracing walk along the cliffs at St Agnes, followed by an inland climb to the top of St Agnes Beacon and an optional coast path walk to the pub.

Cliffs and mines

The awesome sea cliffs of St Agnes Head are well hidden from above. There is no easy view, unless you are a very skilled rock climber. On St Agnes Head and on Carn Gowla, the cliff that runs south from the headland, vast 300ft (91m) high walls of rock soar from an ever restless sea. They do not end at clear-cut edges, however. Instead they merge with gentle slopes of grass and heather that in turn rise gently to the cliff top. Yet you are always aware of the exhilarating exposure of these great gulfs as you stroll safely by.

This walk takes you along the flat cliff top tracks and past the little promontory of Tubby's Head, once an Iron Age settlement fortified by an earth embankment across its neck. From here you pass through what was once an industrious mining landscape, signposted by the remains of mine buildings such as the mighty Towanroath Shaft, a granite castle-keep of a building standing directly above the sea amidst swathes of pink thrift and cream-coloured bladder campion in summer. Built in 1872, this was the pumping house for the Wheal Coates mine whose buildings, further uphill, you see from the coast path. Flooding of the deeper Cornish mines was always a major problem and separate pumping houses were built to draw up water and eject it through tunnels, known as adits, in the cliff face below. The buildings of Towanroath

Trevaunance Cove, north of St Agnes Head, is one of Cornwall's best beaches

Shaft were skilfully restored by the National Trust in the early 1970s.

Beyond Towanroath the path descends into Chapel Porth where you can enjoy the delights of a typical Cornish beach. During the 19th century the entire valley floor that leads down to the cove was given over to the processing of the mineral ore that came from dozens of tin and copper mines, scattered across the surrounding landscape. As you walk up the valley, you pick your way through a landscape now overgrown by nature, but that was once subdued by industry. From the valley floor the route leads up a delightful valley, protected from the harsh onshore weather by high ground. Soon, you climb onto the bare, rounded summit of St Agnes Beacon, 629ft (192m) high and a superb viewpoint. As the name makes clear, this prominent hilltop was used traditionally for the lighting of signal fires and for celebratory bonfires. From the Beacon's airy heights you drop down effortlessly to the coast once more.

the walk

1 Join the coastal footpath from wherever you park along the cliff top. Follow the stony track across **Tubby's Head**. Branch off right onto a narrower path about 100yds (91m) before old mine buildings (these are the remains of Wheal Coates mine). Cross a stone stile and continue to **Towanroath mine engine house**.

2 About 50yds (46m) beyond Towanroath branch off right at a signpost and descend to **Chapel Porth Beach**.

3 Cross the stream at the back corner of the car park and follow a path up **Chapel Coombe** next to the stream. Pass below a mine building and where the path forks among trees, go left through a wooden kissing gate.

4 Cross a **bridge** then turn right onto a track. After a gate and a sharp left-hand bend, bear off right along a grassy track. Pass a house on the left, walk parallel with the **stream**, pass beside a gate and keep alongside a field before turning left over a wooden stile by a gate onto a track. After 50yds (46m), reach a junction with a wide track. Turn left and continue to a public road.

| 3h30 | 7 MILES | 11.3 KM | LEVEL 1 2 3 |

SHORTER ALTERNATIVE ROUTE

| 3h00 | 5 MILES | 8 KM | LEVEL 1 2 3 |

MAP: OS Explorer 104 Redruth & St Agnes

START/FINISH: St Agnes Head. Number of parking places along the clifftop track, grid ref: SW 699512

PATHS: good coastal footpaths and inland tracks

LANDSCAPE: dramatic coastal cliffs and a high heath-covered hill

PUBLIC TOILETS: Chapel Porth

TOURIST INFORMATION: Newquay, tel 01637 854020

THE PUB: Driftwood Spars Hotel, Trevaunance Cove

🔵 Narrow cliff-edge paths, old mine workings and one steady climb to the top of St Agnes Beacon

Getting to the start

St Agnes is on the B3277 and signposted off the A30, 5 miles (8km) north of Redruth at the junction with the A390. In the village centre, turn left opposite the church, then take the third road right in a mile (1.6km) to reach the cliff parking at St Agnes Head.

Researched and written by: David Hancock, Des Hannigan

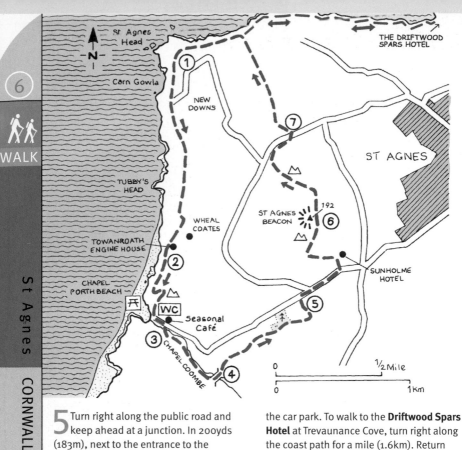

5 Turn right along the public road and keep ahead at a junction. In 200yds (183m), next to the entrance to the **Sunholme Hotel**, continue up a stony track on the left. After 50yds (46m), at a junction, go left and follow a path rising to the obvious summit of **St Agnes Beacon**.

6 From the summit of the Beacon follow the lower of two tracks, heading north west, down towards a road. Just before you reach the road turn right along a narrow path, skirting the base of the hill. Look out for a narrow path left leading downhill, eventually emerging at the road by a seat.

7 Cross over and follow the track opposite, across **New Downs**, directly to the edge of the cliffs, then turn left at a junction with the coast path and return to

the car park. To walk to the **Driftwood Spars Hotel** at Trevaunance Cove, turn right along the coast path for a mile (1.6km). Return along the coast back to the car.

what to look for

In summer the heathery vegetation of the St Agnes cliff tops and the inland hill of the Beacon attract a wealth of butterflies such as the grayling, a brown-coloured butterfly distinguished by the black edges to its wings and the two white-pupilled spots on its fore wings. It feeds on wild thyme and heather and often perches on the rocks. Another butterfly to look out for here is the green hairstreak. It is golden-brown on its upper wings and distinctively green on its under side.

Driftwood Spars Hotel

Constructed in the 17th century of huge ship's timbers and spars (hence the name), with stone and slate, the inn – once a marine chandlery, sail loft and tin miners trading post – is just 100yds (91m) from one of Cornwall's best beaches, making it an ideal family destination. An old smugglers' tunnel completes the picture, while fine views, home-brewed beers and roaring log fires in the atmospheric bars add to the appeal.

Food
Wide-ranging menus take in traditional bar snacks, fresh local fish and seafood and an assortment of Italian, Indian and Greek dishes.

Family facilities
Children of all ages are welcome throughout the inn. Expect to find a children's menu, smaller portions of adult dishes, high chairs and five family bedrooms.

Alternative refreshment stops
There is a seasonal café at Chapel Porth, at the midway point of the walk. St Agnes

village has a couple of good pubs where you can get bar meals.

☞ Where to go from here
Take the ultimate undersea safari at the Blue Reef Aquarium in Newquay. Enjoy close encounters with graceful sharks and rays and stroll among the colourful inhabitants of a coral reef in a spectacular underwater tunnel (www.bluereefaquarium.co.uk). Newquay Zoo is set in exotic lakeside gardens, where monkeys and wallabies roam freely along with otters in the oriental garden. Highlights include feeding time talks, animal encounters, the tropical house and the penguin pool (www.newquayzoo.co.uk).

about the pub

Driftwood Spars Hotel
Trevaunance Cove, St Agnes
Cornwall TR5 0RT
Tel 01872 552428
www.driftwoodspars.com

DIRECTIONS: return to the village centre and turn left along the B3277, then right at the junction with the B3285 and follow signs left for Trevaunance Cove.	
PARKING: 80	
OPEN: daily; all day	
FOOD: daily	
BREWERY/COMPANY: free house	
REAL ALE: Tetley, Sharp's Own and Doom Bar, St Austell HSD, Cuckoo Ale	
DOGS: allowed inside	
ROOMS: 15 en suite	

Around Cadgwith

A wandering route between coast and countryside through the landscape of the Lizard Peninsula.

Serpentine rock

The serpentine rock of the Lizard Peninsula is fascinating. Its geological label, serpentinite fails to slither quite so easily off the tongue as does its popular usage 'serpentine'. The name derives from the sinuous veins of green, red, yellow and white that wriggle across the dark green or brownish red surface of the rock. The best

serpentine is easily carved and shaped and can be polished to a beautiful sheen. In the 19th century serpentine furnishings were the height of fashion but the industry declined during the 1890s. Serpentine became less popular for use in shop fronts and monuments as cheaper, more resilient marble from Italy and Spain began to dominate the market. Today serpentine craftsmen still operate in little workshops on The Lizard and you can buy serpentine souvenirs at Lizard Village. Throughout this walk are stiles built of serpentine whose surfaces are mirror-smooth and slippery. Admire, but take care when they are wet.

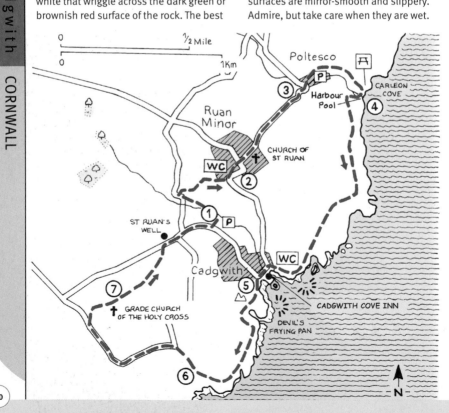

The walk first takes a fittingly wandering route inland to the sleepy village of Ruan Minor from where a narrow lane leads down to the Poltesco Valley. At the mouth of the valley is Carleon Cove, once the site of waterwheels, steam engines, machine shops, storehouses and a factory where serpentine was processed. Only a few ruins remain. A narrow harbour pool, almost stagnant now, is dammed on the seaward side by a deep shingle bank where once there was an outlet to the sea.

From Carleon Cove the coast path is followed pleasantly to Cadgwith, an archetypal Cornish fishing village. Cadgwith has a number of thatched cottages, a rare sight in windy Cornwall, although coverings of wire-mesh on most of them indicate wise precaution against storm damage.

Cadgwith still supports a fleet of small fishing boats and is given an enduring identity because of it. Beyond the village the coast path leads to the Devil's Frying Pan, a vast gulf in the cliffs caused by the collapse of a section of coast. From here the path leads on for a short distance along the edge of the cliffs before the route turns inland to the Church of the Holy Cross at Grade. Two fields beyond the church you find the ancient St Ruan's Well and the road that leads back to the start of this ramble.

the walk

1 Go left along a grassy ride below the **car park,** to a stile. Cross a field, then branch right through a gate to join a wooded path. Turn right at a lane, cross

The sea bubbles and fizzes at the Devil's Frying Pan at Cadgwith

2h00	4.5 MILES	7.2 KM	LEVEL 1 2 3

MAP: OS Explorer 103 The Lizard

START/FINISH: Cadgwith car park, about 350yds (320m) from Cadgwith. Busy in summer; grid ref: SW 719146

PATHS: very good, coast path occasionally rocky in places, field paths

LANDSCAPE: landlocked lanes and woodland tracks, coastal footpaths high above the sea

PUBLIC TOILETS: Ruan Minor and Cadgwith

TOURIST INFORMATION: Helston, tel 01326 565431

THE PUB: Cadgwith Cove Inn, Cadgwith Cove

❶ There are two moderate climbs along the coast path and the cliff path can be slippery when wet

Getting to the start

From the A394 at Helston take the A3083 south, signposted 'The Lizard'. After 8 miles (12.9km) turn left for Cadgwith and follow signs for the car park. Avoid entering the village as the lanes are very steep and narrow.

Researched and written by: David Hancock, Des Hannigan

a bridge then, on the corner by the **postbox**, go up the track ahead. Turn right at an unsigned junction and continue to the main road at **Ruan Minor**.

2 Go left and, just beyond the shop, turn left down a surfaced path. Rejoin the main road by a **thatched cottage** (there are toilets just before the road). Cross diagonally right, then go down a lane past the Church of St Ruan.

3 Just past an **old mill** and a bridge, go right at a T-junction to reach the car park at **Poltesco**. From the far end of the car park follow a track, signposted 'Carleon Cove'. Go right at a junction.

4 Turn left at a T-junction just above the cove and again turn left where the path branches in about 0.25 mile (400m). Continue along the cliff-edge path to **Cadgwith**.

5 Follow a narrow path, signposted 'Coast Path'. By a house gateway, go left up a surfaced path, signposted '**Devil's Frying Pan**'. At an open area turn left, pass Townplace Cottage, cross a meadow and reach the Devil's Frying Pan itself.

The village of Cadgwith perches on steep slopes. Thatched buildings are of local serpentine rock

6 At a junction, just past a chalet studio, follow a path inland to a T-junction with a rough track. Turn left and, at a public lane, go left again to reach the entrance to **Grade church**, after 1 mile (1.6km). Go through the gate to the church.

7 Follow the field edge behind the church, then cross the next field to reach a lane. **St Ruan's Well** is opposite diagonally left. Turn right for 200yds (183m), then branch off right between **stone pillars** to return to the car park.

what to look for

The Church of St Ruan is a small, endearing building built mainly of local serpentine stone. It has a low tower, as if bitten off by the notorious Lizard wind. The east window is dedicated to Thomas Richard Collinson Harrison, a 16 year old who died in a cliff fall in 1909. Grade Church stands on raised ground above flood-prone fields. It is a raw, but atmospheric building that can be satisfyingly gloomy and primeval on dull days and at dusk.

Cadgwith Cove Inn

Whitewashed 300-year-old smugglers' inn set right on the Lizard coastal path overlooking the old pilchard cellars and the colourful fishing vessels on the steep shingle beach in this attractive cove. Virtually unchanged since the old smuggling days, the two rustic bars are simply furnished and each has a warming winter fire. Relics of bygone seafaring days adorn the walls, including prints and photographs of old fishermen and scenes of Cadgwith many years ago. The half-panelled lounge bar opens out onto a sun-trap patio with wooden benches, the ideal meeting place for walkers seeking a pint of Sharp's ale and the best crab sandwich for miles.

Food

Seafood is a speciality, with crab landed on the beach appearing in sandwiches, soups and salads, as well as local fish and chips, fish casserole and lobster in season. Alternatives include ploughman's lunches, lasagne, meat pies and steaks.

Family facilities

There's a specified family area where children are welcome. Smaller portions of some of the main menu dishes are available, while younger family members can choose from the children's menu.

about the pub

Cadgwith Cove Inn
Cadgwith, Helston
Cornwall TR12 7JX
Tel 01326 290513
www.cadgwithcoveinn.com

DIRECTIONS: see Getting to the start; pub in village above cove

PARKING: use village car park

OPEN: daily; all day Saturday and Sunday, and July and August

FOOD: daily

BREWERY/COMPANY: Punch Taverns

REAL ALE: Flowers IPA, Sharp's Doom Bar, guest beer

DOGS: allowed inside

ROOMS: 7 bedrooms, 2 en suite

Alternative refreshment stops

The Old Cellars Restaurant in Cadgwith is licensed and features the courtyard of old pilchard processing 'cellars' right opposite Cadgwith harbour beach.

☛ Where to go from here

Visit the Goonhilly Satellite Earth Station Experience near Helston. Here you can journey through the history of international satellite and radio communications in the Connected Earth Gallery, discover the interactive exhibition area and take a guided tour of the site, getting closer to the massive satellite dishes (www.goonhilly.bt.com).

Helford Estuary

A circuit of some of the peaceful tidal creeks of the Helford Estuary.

Helford CORNWALL

Helford

The Helford River is enduringly popular with land-based visitors and leisure sailors alike, yet the area manages somehow to absorb it all. Cars probe tentatively between the unforgiving stone hedges of narrow Cornish lanes. The bulk of river craft are yachts, so that on a busy sailing day you will hear only the pleasing flap of sails blowing through, as flocks of vessels tack across the estuary mouth. The pelt of trees that lines the estuary and its subsidiary creeks plays a great part in this muffling of too much human racket.

Yet the picturesque, leisure-dominated Helford of today was once a bustling haven for all sorts of trade and, not least, was a haven for pirates and smugglers. During Elizabethan times especially, a passel of Cornish rascals, from the highest in the land to the lowest, was engaged in plundering the cargoes of vessels that sailed through the Channel approaches. The Helford, as it is popularly known, was a secretive, useful base from which all manner of goods could be spirited away inland. In later times the river became an equally secretive base for missions against German-occupied France during the Second World War.

There is little physical evidence of any of this busy past, but in the shrouded creeks that run off like fibrous roots from the main river it is easy to imagine the utter remoteness of life hundreds of years ago, when movement by sea was far more convenient than by land. This walk starts from the village of Helford and follows the southern shore of the estuary between Treath and Dennis Head, mainly through the deep woodland of the Bosahan estate. There are tantalising glimpses of the river through the trees and the path skirts tiny coves such as Bosahan and Ponsence with their inviting beaches that must surely have seen their share of night-landings in the piratical past.

The return leg of the walk follows the north shore of the adjacent Gillan Creek, far smaller and thus far less accommodating to vessels than the deep Helford. Here the tiny Church of St Anthony adds to the overall serenity. From near the head of the creek, you climb inland to Manaccan, a charming hamlet that seems to tumble down the slopes of the valley. Beyond the village the route leads into the wooded valley above Helford and takes you back to your starting point through chequered shade.

the walk

1 As you leave the car park, turn left along a path, signed '**Coast Path**'. Go through a metal gate and follow a sunken track. Descend steps, then turn right along a lane. At a steep right-hand bend, bear off ahead along a track. Pass behind a house and follow this permissive path through trees, keeping left at any junctions.

3h00 · 5 MILES · 8 KM · LEVEL 123

WALK

2 Leave the wooded area via a **metal gate**, then turn left along a field edge to a stone stile, Follow the bottom edge of the next two fields. Go through a field gap beside a **white pole** and a post with orange triangle (these are navigation marks). Follow the field edge ahead. Go through a kissing gate, then follow the field edge (there's a seat and **viewpoint** on the left), to where it ends at the beginning of a wide track (to make the short circuit of **Dennis Head**, follow the track ahead to a stile on the left).

3 To continue on the main route, turn sharply right at the start of the wide track and follow the left-hand field edge and then a path across the open field. Join a track behind a house, then go through a kissing gate and descend to **St Anthony's Church**. Follow the road alongside Gillan Creek,

The village of Helford on the Helford Estuary

MAP: OS Explorer 103 The Lizard

START/FINISH: Helford village car park (can become busy in summer); grid ref: SW 759261

PATHS: good woodland paths and tracks, field paths, short section of quiet lane, 9 stiles

LANDSCAPE: wooded creekside and fields

PUBLIC TOILETS: at start

TOURIST INFORMATION: Helston, tel 01326 565431

THE PUB: Shipwright's Arms, Helford

Getting to the start

Take the A3083 south from Helston towards the Lizard, then turn left along the B3293 for St Keverne. Turn left in 2.5 miles (4km) for Newtown St Martin and follow signs for Manaccan and Helford. Park in the village car park.

Researched and written by:
David Hancock, Des Hannigan

Helford

4 Just past where the road curves round a bay, go up right through a gate by a public footpath sign. Follow a broad track through trees to houses at **Roscaddon**. Keep ahead along a track that leads to **Manaccan** at a T-junction opposite Manaccan church.

5 Go through the **churchyard** and on through the gate opposite to a road (the village shop is to the left). Keep ahead to a junction, the **New Inn** is down to the left, then go up right, past the school. Keep uphill, then turn left along **Minster Meadow**, go over a stile, and through fields to reach a road.

6 Go diagonally left to the stile opposite, cross a field, then go left following signposts to reach **woods**. Follow the path ahead. At a junction keep ahead, go over a stile and reach a second junction.

7 Bear right and follow a broad track through trees. Continue ahead at a further junction to reach some buildings at **Helford**. Keep ahead on reaching a surfaced road and follow the road up to the car park.

what to look for

There are two churches on the route of the walk, St Anthony-in-Meneage and St Manacca at Manaccan. Both have some fine features. At St Anthony the piers of the single aisle lean engagingly to port; the 15th-century font has fine reliefs of angels holding shields. Look for the granite drinking bowl, complete with engaging inscription, outside the main door. Manaccan's church has a splendid Norman south door. The church also has a single arcade, but its wagon roofs are well-renovated. There is an ancient fig tree growing out of the wall.

Shipwright's Arms

Superbly situated on the banks of the Helford River in an idyllic village setting, this small thatched pub is especially popular in summer when customers can relax on the three delightful terraces, complete with palm trees and colourful flowers, which lead down to the water's edge. The pub was built in 1795 as a farmhouse with later shipwright connections and attracts the yachting fraternity as well as visitors to this charming coastal spot. If it's raining the interior is equally as special. It is traditional and unspoilt with a black panelled bar, a large wood-burning stove and a wealth of nautical artefacts, from a ship's wheel to a display of knots and drawings of local fishermen on the walls.

Food

The summer buffet offers crab and lobster, alongside various ploughman's lunches, salads, home-made pies, marinated lamb fillet and local steaks. Barbecues in summer on the terrace.

Family facilities

Although there are no specific family facilities, children are welcome inside the pub.

Alternative refreshment stops

There's a small café at the sailing shop in St Anthony, the New Inn at Manaccan and a tearoom in Helford.

☞ Where to go from here

Take the passenger ferry across the river and visit the sheltered sub-tropical garden at Glendurgan. Children will love exploring the famous laurel maze and the Giant's Stride (www.nationaltrust.org.uk). Visit the National Seal Sanctuary at Gweek for a unique opportunity to learn more about these beautiful creatures (www.sealsanctuary.co.uk). At Flambards Village Theme Park explore a recreated Victorian village street, Britain in the Blitz, and the Science Centre, a science playground for the whole family, and enjoy exhilarating rides and other attractions (www.flambards.co.uk).

about the pub

Shipwright's Arms
Helford, Helston
Cornwall TR12 6JX
Tel 01326 231235

DIRECTIONS: see Getting to the start; follow village road to the other side of Helford Creek

PARKING: use village car park

OPEN: closed Sunday and Monday evenings in winter

FOOD: daily

BREWERY/COMPANY: free house

REAL ALE: Castle Eden Ale, Greene King IPA, Sharp's Doom Bar

DOGS: allowed in the bar on a lead

Mylor Churchtown to Flushing

From Mylor Churchtown to Flushing in a quiet peninsula world still dominated by ships and sails.

The Carrick roads

The inner estuary of the River Fal is reputedly the world's third largest natural harbour. It has welcomed vessels from Tudor warships to fishing fleets, to modern cargo vessels and oil rigs and a growing number of yachts. Part of the long maritime heritage of the Fal belongs to the Post Office Packet Service, which managed communications throughout the British Empire from the Fal between 1689 and 1850. Fast Packet vessels ran south to Spain and Portugal and on to the Americas. The Packet sailors were notorious for their opportunism and many a Packetship returned from a trip with more than half its cargo as contraband. The main Packet base was at Falmouth, but Mylor was a servicing and victualling yard for the Packet boats. Many Packet captains lived at Flushing in what was effectively maritime suburbia.

At Mylor today boatyards still bustle with work and local sailing clubs thrive. Double Olympic sailing gold medal winner Ben Ainslie, learned many of his skills as a Laser dinghy sailor here and today every creek and inlet of the Fal is dense with sailing and leisure craft. Modern Flushing is an exquisitely peaceful backwater, within shouting distance of bustling Falmouth, but with the river between.

The walk takes you from Mylor along the shores of the blunt headland between Mylor Creek and the Penryn River and on to Flushing, in full view of Falmouth docks.

Flushing is an enclave of handsome houses, many with Dutch features. At Point 4 on the walk, note the plaque commemorating the Post Office Packet Service. From Flushing you turn inland and on to a delightful old track that runs down a wooded valley to Mylor Creek from where quiet lanes lead back to St Mylor Church. Here in a churchyard that resonates with maritime history, stands the Ganges Memorial to 53 youngsters who died, mainly of disease, on the famous Royal Naval training ship HMS *Ganges*, which was based at Mylor from 1866 to 1899.

the walk

1 From the car park entrance at **Mylor Churchtown**, turn right to the start of a surfaced walkway, signposted to Flushing. Follow the walkway then, by the gateway of a house, bear left along a path signposted to Flushing. Pass in front of **Restronguet Sailing Club**, go up some steps and turn left along the coast path.

2 Follow the path round **Penarrow Point** and continue round Trefusis Point. Reach a gate and granite grid stile by a wooden shack at **Kilnquay Wood**. Continue to a lane.

3 Follow the surfaced lane round left, then go right through a gap beside a

Left: Mylor has a strong maritime heritage
Below: Fishermen unload at Flushing

2h00	4 MILES	6.4 KM	LEVEL 1 2 3

MAP: OS Explorer 105 Falmouth & Mevagissey

START/FINISH: Mylor Churchtown pay-and-display car park; grid ref: SW 820352

PATHS: good paths throughout. Wooded section to Trelew Farm is often very wet, 5 stiles

LANDSCAPE: wooded peninsula flanked by river estuaries and creeks

PUBLIC TOILETS: Mylor Churchtown and Flushing

TOURIST INFORMATION: Falmouth, tel 01326 312300

THE PUB: The Seven Stars Inn, Flushing

Getting to the start

Mylor Churchtown lies east of Penryn and is best reached from the A39 north of Falmouth. In Penryn follow signs along narrow lanes for Flushing and Mylor Churchtown for 3 miles (4.8km). Pass the Church of St Mylor to the waterfront and marina and turn right into the car park.

Researched and written by:
David Hancock, Des Hannigan

gate and continue along a public road. Where the road drops down towards the water's edge, bear right up a surfaced slope to reach the delightful grassy area of the **'Bowling Green'**. (Strictly no dog fouling please.) Continue past a little pavilion and toilets and go down a surfaced walkway, then turn left by a junction and signpost into **Flushing**.

4 Turn right at a street junction and go along Trefusis Road past The Seven Stars Inn. At a junction by the Royal Standard Inn, keep right past the **post office** and go up Kersey Road. At the top of the road, by Orchard Vale, go left up steps, signposted **'Mylor Church'**. Cross a stile and keep to the field edge to reach an isolated house and to a stile made of **granite bollards**.

5 In a few paces go right across a stile then turn left over a cattle grid and follow the drive to a public road, **Penarrow Road**. Cross with care and go down the road opposite for 30yds (27m), then go right down steps and on down the field edge. Keep straight ahead where the field edge bends left, and enter shady **woods**.

6 Enter the woodland and keep right at a junction to follow a rocky path that is often a mini stream after heavy rainfall. Go through a gate, keep left at a junction then

cross a proper **stream**. Go through a gate and continue on the narrow path to a tiny gate. Turn right down a farm track to reach a surfaced lane at **Trelew**.

7 Turn right along the lane, passing an old water pump. When you get to a slipway, keep ahead along the unsurfaced **Wayfield Road**. Continue along between granite posts and on to join the public road into Mylor Churchtown. Cross the road with care (this is a blind corner) and go through the churchyard of **St Mylor Church** (note that the path through the churchyard is not a public right of way). Turn right when you reach the **waterfront** to find the car park.

what to look for

The wooded sections of the walk are composed mainly of deciduous trees. Unlike conifer woods, these diverse environments support numerous flowering plants amidst their damp, tangled, humus-rich undergrowth. Look for the pink and red flowers of herb Robert and campion and the starry white blooms of greater stitchwort. This latter plant was believed to have curative properties in earlier times; it was ground into a paste and applied to boils and sores. Children in Cornwall were once warned not to touch stitchwort at night or they would become 'pixie-led' and lost in the woods.

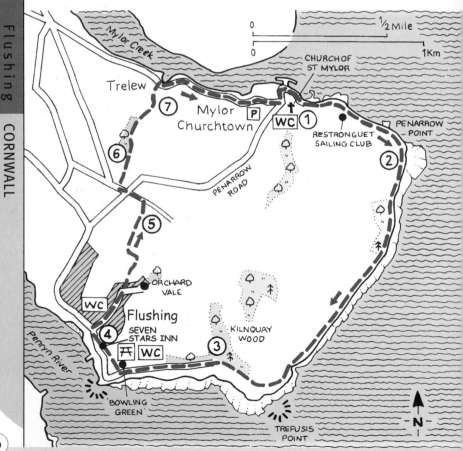

The Seven Stars Inn

Standing opposite a tiny harbour with views across the Penryn River to Falmouth Docks, the unpretentious Seven Stars is a popular free house and the hub of village life. Sit at well-placed front tables in summer or retreat in winter into the large and well furnished main bar for pints of Cornish ale and daily fish specialities. There's a separate restaurant to the rear and a games room with pool table.

Food

From lunchtime sandwiches and traditional light pub meals the menu extends to excellent fish from local boats, perhaps megrim sole, sea bass, cod or plaice. Crab, lamb and beef also feature on the restaurant menu.

Family facilities

Children are welcome inside the pub and young children have their own menu.

Alternative refreshment stops

Also at the halfway point at Flushing is the Royal Standard Inn. At Mylor Bridge there is a café and restaurant on the waterfront.

☞ Where to go from here

Head for Discovery Quay in Falmouth and the exciting, award-winning National Maritime Museum Cornwall (www.nmmc.co.uk). You can discover Cornwall's maritime heritage, learn to sail inside by mastering model boats on the 40ft (12m) pool, explore hands-on exhibits and the Tidal Zone, which offers a unique fish eye view of life under the water. You can also take in the breathtaking view across Falmouth's harbour from a 95ft (29m) lookout tower. Along the A394 towards Helston is the Poldark Mine and Heritage Complex which explains the history of tin production in Cornwall from 1800 BC through to the 19th century. Take a guided tour of the mine workings and pan for gold (www.poldark-mine.com).

about the pub

The Seven Stars Inn
3 Trefusis Road, Flushing,
Falmouth, Cornwall TR11 5TY
Tel 01326 374373

DIRECTIONS: see Getting to the start. Follow signs to Flushing; pub in the village centre, opposite the river; Point 4 on walk
PARKING: none
OPEN: daily; all day
FOOD: daily; no food Sunday evening in winter
BREWERY/COMPANY: free house
REAL ALE: Skinner's Betty Stogs, Keel Over and Cornish Knocker
DOGS: allowed inside on leads

To Nare Head and Veryan

A coastal and field walk through some of South Cornwall's more remote and endearing landscapes.

Remote Cornish coast

There are parts of the Cornish coast that seem especially remote, where main roads have been kept at arms' length and where human development has not gone beyond farming and small scale sea-going. The lonely stretch of South Cornish coast between Gerrans Bay and Veryan Bay,

with Nare Head at its centre, is one such place, a landscape where people seem to have lived always at a healthy distance from too much intrusion.

The walk begins at the seasonally popular Carne Beach. A steady hike along the coast path from here soon brings you to a steep descent into the narrow Paradoe, pronounced 'Perada', Cove. On a spur of land above the sea is the ruin of a small cottage. This was the home of a 19th-century fisherman called Mallet, who lived during the week in this lonely spot, fishing from 'Mallet's Cove' below. He then

returned at weekends to his wife at the village of Veryan, a few miles inland. Eventually Mallet emigrated to Australia – without his wife. Weekends had become non-negotiable, perhaps. The little ruined cottage above the restless sea still speaks of a life of extraordinary detachment.

From Paradoe it is a long, punishing climb to the flat top of Nare Head. Beyond the Head a pleasant ramble takes you along the coast past the steep Rosen Cliff and by lonely coves. Offshore lies the formidable Gull Rock. You soon head inland from this into a lost world of little fields and meadows that straggle across country to Veryan.

From Veryan the route wanders back towards the sea, past the ancient landmark of Carne Beacon, a Bronze Age burial site that saw later service as a signal station, as a triangulation point and as a Second World War observation post. Before these later uses, the bones beneath had been disturbed by curious Victorians. A few fields away lies 'Veryan Castle', known also as 'The Ringarounds', the site of a late Iron Age farming settlement. These ancient sites prove that this absorbing landscape has given refuge to people for thousands of years. From the high ground the route leads down to the coast once more.

the walk

1 Turn left out of the car park and walk up the road, with care. Just past the steep bend, turn off right and go up steps and onto the coast path. Follow the coast path to **Paradoe Cove** and then begin the long climb up to Nare Head. Continue to **Rosen Cliff** with good views of Gull Rock.

3h00 · **5 MILES** · **8 KM** · **LEVEL 1 2 3**

MAP: OS Explorer 105 Falmouth & Mevagissey
START/FINISH: Carne Beach National Trust car park; grid ref: SW 906384
PATHS: good coastal footpath, field paths, quiet lanes, 18 stiles (field stiles are often overgrown)
LANDSCAPE: vegetated coast with some cliffs, mainly flat fields on inland section
PUBLIC TOILETS: Carne Beach, Veryan
TOURIST INFORMATION: Truro, tel 01872 274555
THE PUB: The New Inn, Veryan
❶ The coast path can be slippery after rain. Steep sections of coast/cliff path make the early stages of this walk suitable only for older, fitter children

Getting to the start
From the A39 east of Truro take the A3078 for Tregony and St Mawes. Pass through Tregony then, at a junction by a petrol station, turn left for Veryan. Follow signs into the village, pass the church and the New Inn, following signs for the Nare Hotel. Continue for 2 miles (3.2km), pass the hotel and drop down to Carne Beach and the car park.

Researched and written by:
David Hancock, Des Hannigan

what to look for

Veryan is one of South Cornwall's most fascinating villages. It is famous for its five whitewashed round houses with thatched conical roofs. They date from the early 19th century and were the inspiration of the Revd Jeremiah Trist, a local landowner. Various fanciful myths attach to these houses but they seem to have simply reflected a contemporary fashion for ornamental architecture. Gull Rock, the steep-sided island that lies a short distance offshore from Nare Head is a seabird colony and it has belonged to the National Trust since 1989. The rock's seabirds were exploited for centuries, their eggs were harvested for food, a precarious exercise because the bulk of seabirds nest on the sheer, land-facing cliff. The birds themselves were also trapped and shot for food. In its time Gull Rock even featured as a location for the 1950s film Treasure Island. Gull Rock is now a secure nesting site for guillemots, kittiwakes, herring gulls, cormorants and shags.

2 Above **Kiberick Cove** go through a gap in a wall and turn sharply left to follow a path uphill through scrub and round to the right to reach a stile by a gate into a lane end. Turn right and follow the lane inland to reach a right-hand bend just past a house.

3 Go left and over a **wall stile** here, follow the left edge of a field, then go over another stile on the left. Bear half-right across the next field to reach a gate, then turn right and follow the right-hand field edge to cross two stiles to reach a road. Turn left.

4 Just past **Tregamenna Manor Farm**, on a bend, go over a stile by a gate. Cut across the corner of the field, then go right over a stile. Cross the next field towards houses to a stile and then continue to a T-junction with a lane. Turn right to visit Veryan and **The New Inn**.

5 Return back up the lane, between the two thatched round houses then, just past **Churchtown Farm**, go left again over a stile. Follow the edge of the field to a stile into a lane. (To visit Veryan Castle, turn right along the lane to reach the access path to the castle on the left.) Go immediately left over two stiles, then follow a path, past **Carne Beacon**, to a lane.

6 At a corner junction keep ahead down the lane, signposted 'Carne Village Only'. Bear right down a driveway past **Beacon Cottage**. Go through the gate signposted 'Defined Footpaths Nos 44 & 45'. Follow the track round to the right past a garage, then follow a grassy track, keeping ahead at a junction signposted '**Carne Beach**'. Go through a gate (put dogs on leads here please) and follow a path alongside a grassy bank and fence.

7 Abreast of an old wooden gate up on the right, bear away left and downhill through the scrub, (the path isn't evident at first), and soon pick up a path that leads through gorse to join the coast path back to Carne Beach and the **car park**.

Veryan is known for its round houses

The New Inn

Set in a sleepy village in the heart of the unspoilt Roseland Peninsula, close to safe sandy beaches and St Mawes, the New Inn was formerly two early 18th-century cottages before being converted into a pub. Inside the whitewashed stone exterior is a single carpeted bar, which is delightfully simple, with stone fireplaces, one with a wood-burning stove, warming either end of the long beamed room. Polished brasses and tankards adorn the bar and old photographs of the village line the walls. Upstairs there are three en suite bedrooms.

Food

Simple, satisfying dishes range from lunchtime pasta meals, ham, egg and chips, cottage pie, home-made pizzas, ploughman's lunches and filled rolls.

Evening additions include sea bass with pesto, lamb shank, fillet steak with Stilton sauce and specials like whole lemon sole.

Family facilities

Children of all ages are allowed in the pub and smaller portions of the main menu dishes are served. Secluded rear garden.

Alternative refreshment stops

The Tregarthen Coffee Shop, part of the Elerkey Guest House, is in Veryan.

☛ Where to go from here

St Mawes has a very pretty harbourside and estuary views, a long waterfront to stroll along and a remarkably well preserved 16th-century castle to visit (www.english-heritage.org.uk). Take the King Harry Ferry across the Fal estuary to see the beautifully kept gardens at Trelissick, set in 500 acres (202ha) of riverside parkland (www.nationaltrust.org.uk), or head east to explore the fully restored Lost Gardens of Heligan near Mevagissey (www.heligan.com).

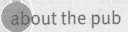

about the pub

The New Inn
Veryan, Truro
Cornwall TR2 5QA
Tel 01872 501362
www.veryan44.freeserve.co.uk

DIRECTIONS:	see Getting to the start
PARKING:	roadside parking
OPEN:	daily
FOOD:	daily
BREWERY/COMPANY:	St Austell Brewery
REAL ALE:	St Austell Tinner's Ale, HSD and Tribute
DOGS:	not allowed inside
ROOMS:	3 bedrooms; 2 en suite

The Camel Trail – Edmonton to Padstow

Fabulous views and wonderful birdlife make this section of the Camel Trail a delight at any time of year.

Padstow and Prideaux Place

Although Padstow is frequently almost overrun with visitors – especially so since chef Rick Stein took up residence – it is still an attractive little town with an interesting maritime history. St Petroc is said to have come here from Wales in the 6th century AD and founded a monastery which was later sacked by the Vikings in the 10th century. The name Padstow comes from 'Petroc stow' (Petroc's church). Being the only

decent harbour on the north coast between Bude and St Ives, Padstow was once the fourth most important port in the country, exporting copper and tin, slate and farm produce. Padstow's famous ancient and pagan Obby Oss ceremony takes place every year on May Day. Rumour has it that it even deterred a party of raiding Frenchmen during the Hundred Years' War!

The Prideaux family – whose origins date back to the 11th century – built their home, Prideaux Place, above the town in the 16th century, and their descendants still live there. This beautiful Elizabethan mansion – now open to the public – is surrounded by gardens laid out in Georgian and Victorian times. A tunnel, giving the

Right: Padstow Harbour
Below left: Taking a break on The Camel Trail

| 2h00 | 10 MILES | 16.1 KM | LEVEL 2 |

family private access, leads from the grounds to St Petroc's Church.

the ride

1 The Quarryman Inn is a fascinating place. Behind the pub are two terraces of stone cottages, originally homes for workers at the quarries (Point 3); when these fell into disuse in the early 20th century the building became a TB isolation hospital. Today it is a very welcoming pub. From the **car park** turn right. At the crossroads turn left and enjoy a lovely downhill run, with increasingly good views over the River Camel and rolling farmland beyond. The Camel was known as the Allen river until 1870, thought to derive from the Irish word alaln, for beautiful: it's clear to see why. Pass through the hamlet at **Tregunna** and follow the lane over a bridge to its end. Turn right down a narrow earthy path to reach the trail

2 Turn right and follow the trail along the edge of the **estuary**. At low tide it's almost like cycling along the edge of a beach as the river is flanked by broad expanses of sand and the views are superb. The creeks and sandbanks attract wintering wildfowl – widgeon, goldeneye, long tailed duck – as well as many divers and waders, spring and autumn migrants. Look out for curlew, oystercatcher, shelduck and little egret. One of the main reasons for constructing the railway was to transport sea sand, rich in lime, from the estuary, to fertilise farmland away from the coast. Granite, slate, tin, iron and copper from mines on Bodmin Moor were exported.

MAP: OS Explorer 106 Newquay & Padstow

START/FINISH: The Quarryman Inn, Edmonton; grid ref: SW 964727

TRAILS/TRACKS: well-surfaced former railway track

LANDSCAPE: river estuary, rolling farmland

PUBLIC TOILETS: Padstow

TOURIST INFORMATION: Padstow, tel 01841 533449

CYCLE HIRE: Camel Trail Cycle Hire, Wadebridge, tel 01208 814104

THE PUB: The Quarryman Inn, Edmonton

🛈 Padstow is very busy at holiday times – leave your bikes at the secure lock-up on the quay and go into town on foot

Getting to the start

Edmonton is west of Wadebridge. Bypass Wadebridge on the A39 signed 'St Columb Major/Padstow'. About 1 mile (1.6km) after crossing the Camel turn right, before Whitecross, on a lane signed 'Edmonton'

Why do this cycle ride?

If you prefer to avoid Wadebridge, try this route to access the lower part of the Camel Trail. It is busier than the Dunmere to Wadebridge stretch, but the views make it worthwhile, and starting from the Quarryman's Arms is a bonus. If you want to keep away from crowds of people, turn round on the edge of Padstow, or just dive in quickly for an ice cream. If you like birdlife don't forget your binoculars.

Researched and written by: Sue Viccars

Map labels:

Rock • Splatt
Prideaux Place •
Porthilly
ferries
0 ½ mile
0 ½ km
B3314
B3276
90 ▲ Trevelver
P
Padstow
River Camel
6
obelisk • 5
CAMEL TRAIL
Cant Hill ▲ 75
3
quarries (disused)
CAMEL TRAIL
A389
Little Petherick Creek
Tregonce
P
4
Pinkson Creek
2
Tregunna
Trevorrick
Quarryman Inn
Edmonton
–N–
Bodellick
Tregonna
START P
1
Penhale
Wadebridge
Little Petherick
Trevance
Whitecross
B3274
St Issey
A389
130 ▲
A39

---

3 A long cutting ends at the spoil heaps of the old slate quarries, with rounded, wooded **Cant Hill** opposite. The estuary is widening as it approaches the sea; there's a glimpse of **Padstow** ahead on the left bank. The mouth of the Camel Estuary is marred by the notorious Doom Bar, a shifting sandbank responsible for more than 300 shipwrecks from 1760 to 1920. If you're cycling the Camel Trail on a sunny day it's hard to imagine such disasters.

4 Continue past **Pinkson Creek** – you may see herons – and continue on to pass the parking area at **Oldtown Cove**. Once through the next cutting you'll get fantastic views towards Rock, on the other side of the estuary, with Brea Hill and Daymer Bay beyond, and out to the open sea. The trail bears away from the estuary through a cutting.

5 Cross the bridge over **Little Petherick Creek**. The Saints' Way, a 30-mile (48km) walking route, links Fowey on the south coast with Padstow's St Petroc's Church. It runs along the edge of the creek and past the **obelisk** (commemorating Queen Victoria's jubilee in 1887) on Dennis Hill, seen ahead. The creek is also an important habitat for little egret and a good range of wading birds.

6 Follow the trail past a lake on the left and then past houses on the edge of Padstow, with moored boats on the water right. **Rock**, opposite, is a popular sailing and watersports venue, and there's always masses to watch on the water. The trail ends at the **quay** and car park; you should dismount at this point to explore the town. Retrace your tracks along the Camel Trail to Edmonton.

The Quarryman Inn

You can expect a genuine warm welcome at this 18th-century village inn that evolved around a carefully reconstructed slate-built courtyard of old quarrymen's cottages. Gas heaters warm this area on cooler days and it is a lovely sheltered spot to enjoy a drink or evening meal. Among the features at this unusual pub are several bow windows, one is a delightful stained-glass quarryman panel, and interesting old brass optics above the fireplace in the beamed bar. Tip-top ale comes from local small breweries and the menu includes fresh local fish.

Food

At lunch tuck into roast ham sandwiches or filled Italian bread (smoked bacon, Brie and cranberry), Cornish fish pie or the curry of the day. Evening additions include tempura prawns with sweet chilli sauce, oven-roasted lamb shank, roast duck with cherry sauce and local fish such as whole bass stuffed with bacon.

Family facilities

Children of all ages are welcome in the pub. Smaller portions of adult meals are available and younger family members have their own menu to choose from.

Alternative refreshment stops

You'll be spoilt for choice in Padstow as there are some good pubs and cafés and a few excellent restaurants.

☛ Where to go from here

Visit the Delabole Slate Quarry near Camelford, the oldest and largest working slate quarry in England. There are tours every weekday (www.delaboleslate.com). Camelford is also the location for the nation's foremost museum of cycling history, from 1818 to the present day, with over 400 cycles, cycling medals and displays of gas lighting. Overlooking the wild Cornish coast are the 13th-century ruins of Tintagel Castle, the legendary birthplace of King Arthur and home to Merlin the magician (www.english-heritage.org.uk). Close to Padstow is the Crealy Adventure Park where kids can scare themselves on the Haunted Castle ride, the Raging River Watercoaster and the Thunder Falls (www.crealy.co.uk).

about the pub

The Quarryman Inn
Edmonton, Wadebridge
Cornwall PL27 7JA
Tel 01208 816444

DIRECTIONS: see Getting to the start
PARKING: 100
OPEN: daily; all day
FOOD: daily
BREWERY/COMPANY: free house
REAL ALE: Skinner's & Sharp's beers, Timothy Taylor Landlord, guest beers

The Camel Trail – Dunmere to Wadebridge

Enjoy a quiet and easy section of the Camel Trail along the lovely wooded banks of the River Camel.

Bodmin Moor

The River Camel rises on Bodmin Moor. Like Dartmoor, over the county boundary in Devon, it is a raised granite plateaux, part of the same huge belt of ancient rock that outcrops to form Penwith in west Cornwall and the Isles of Scilly off Land's End.

Bodmin and Dartmoor are characterised by the presence of tors, heavily weathered outcrops of granite: Bodmin's most famous is the Cheesewring. The highest point on the moors is Brown Willy (1,368ft/417m) and many of Cornwall's beautiful rivers rise on the boggy moorland heights. An old name for this upland tract was 'Fowey Moor' – the source of the River Fowey lies just below Brown Willy. There is evidence of extensive Bronze Age occupation, in the form of megalithic chambered tombs, standing stones and stone circles dating back over 4,000 years. Tin and copper were mined on the moor from the mid 18th century, and china clay – one of

Cornwall's most important sources of wealth – was mined from 1862 until 2001. Bodmin Moor is also recorded for posterity in Daphne du Maurier's classic novel *Jamaica Inn*.

the ride

1 The Camel Trail is clearly accessed from the car park. Push your bike down the steep ramp to join the **old railway track**. A granite block displays a map of the 17-mile (27.4km) trail from Poley's Bridge to Padstow. The railway line from Wadebridge to Dunmere Junction, and then to Bodmin is the third in the country, and the first steam-hauled railway in Cornwall (others used horse power). The Wadebridge to Padstow line opened in 1889 and closed in 1967. Turn left, soon crossing the **River Camel**, which reaches the sea at Padstow.

2h00 | 10 MILES | 16.1 KM | LEVEL 1 23

2 Continue on past the end of the Bodmin and Wenford Steam Railway at **Boscarne Junction**. Boscarne Junction was linked to the main line at Bodmin Road (now Parkway) in 1888. Pass round a staggered barrier and over a small lane; continue through **woodland**.

3 Cross the next lane via a gate (a left turn here will take you to **Nanstallon**, site of a Roman fort); you'll see the Camel Trail Tea Garden on the right. Cycle past access to the **Camel Valley Vineyard** (right) and continue through pretty, mixed woodland – oak, ash, beech, spindle, hazel and holly – with glimpses of the River Camel through the trees left. Pass **Grogley Halt,** where there are picnic tables and access to the river (popular with salmon fishermen here) on the left.

Below: Taking a break on The Camel Trail

MAP: OS Explorer 109 Bodmin Moor and 106 Newquay & Padstow

START/FINISH: Camel Trail car park at Dunmere, grid ref: SX 047675

TRAILS/TRACKS: well-surfaced former railway track

LANDSCAPE: wooded river valley

PUBLIC TOILETS: The Platt, Wadebridge

TOURIST INFORMATION: Wadebridge, tel 08701 223337

CYCLE HIRE: Bodmin Cycle Hire, General Station, Bodmin, tel 01208 73555

THE PUB: The Borough Arms, Dunmere

🔴 Busy road through centre of Wadebridge to rejoin the Camel Trail

Getting to the start

Bodmin lies just off the A30. From the centre of town follow signs for Wadebridge, along the A389 (Dunmere Road). After about 1 mile (1.6km) the road drops downhill. The Borough Arms will be seen on the left. Turn left through the car park into the official Camel Trail car park.

Why do this cycle ride?

This is an easy ride along a pretty, wooded section of the old Bodmin to Wadebridge railway line – now the Camel Trail – and you'll be in Wadebridge before you know it. You can extend the ride by passing through the town and rejoining the Camel Trail along the beautiful Camel estuary to Padstow (see The Camel Trail – Edmonton to Padstow).

Researched and written by: Sue Viccars

4 Pass through a cutting and then by beautiful stone and slate cottages at **Polbrock**. Pass under a bridge and look left for access to the riverbank (note cycle racks on the side of the trail). Pass the grass-covered **Shooting Range Platform** on the left. Cross the Camel again: look ahead right to see the edge of Egloshayle, on the west bank of the Camel. The name means 'church on the estuary', and the church tower soon comes into view across the river meadows and reedbeds.

5 Pass under a small bridge to reach **Guineaport Road**. Follow this quiet residential road towards Wadebridge, passing the **old station** on the left (now the John Betjeman Centre – Sir John Betjeman is buried at St Enodoc Church, near Brea Hill on the Camel Estuary). Follow the road as it bears left to reach a roundabout, with the cinema opposite. Turn right down **The Platt** (once regularly flooded so boats were

drawn up here in the 19th century). **Wadebridge**, dating back to the early 14th century and situated at the lowest crossing point of the Camel, makes a good focus for the ride. There are plenty of pubs and cafés, and it's worth taking a look at the much-altered medieval bridge across the Camel, believed by some to have been built on sacks of wool.

6 If you want to keep going on the Camel Trail keep straight ahead at the next roundabout along **Eddystone Road** passing the tourist information (and various cafés) on the right. Granite for the rebuilding of the Eddystone lighthouse, off Plymouth, was shipped from Wadebridge Town Quay. At the next roundabout take the **third exit** (by the bike hire shops) and you'll be back on the Camel Trail again. Return along the trail to the car park and The Borough Arms at Dunmere.

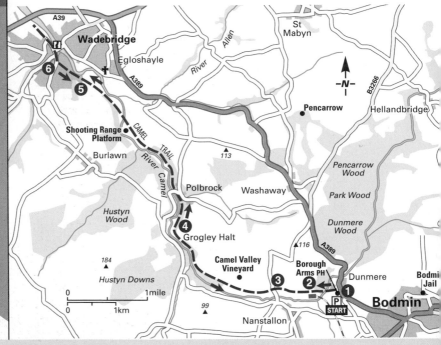

The Borough Arms

Situated in glorious countryside close to Bodmin Moor, this popular pub stands on the route of the Camel Trail and welcomes walkers and cyclists exploring this traffic-free route between Bodmin and Padstow. Much extended over recent years it makes a great spot to rest weary legs and refuel with a pint of Cornish ale and some hearty pub food. There are bike racks in the car park and children, who are really welcome, can explore the adventure playground on fine days.

Food

Traditional pub fare includes a light menu of sandwiches, ploughman's and jacket potatoes. More substantial dishes include steak and ale pie, beer battered cod and chips and lasagne, plus daily specials and a fill-your-own-plate carvery.

Family facilities

Children are allowed in the areas away from the bar and notices inform parents that children must be accompanied at all times. In addition to the family areas, there's a kid's menu, smaller portions of adult meals, high chairs and baby-changing facilities.

Alternative refreshment stops

The Camel Trail Tea Garden at Point 3 and various pubs and cafés in Wadebridge.

☛ Where to go from here

Restored steam locomotives at the Bodmin & Wenford Railway take you back to the glory days of the Great Western Railway when hordes of holidaymakers travelled the route to the sun

about the pub

The Borough Arms
Dunmere, Bodmin
Cornwall PL31 2RD
Tel 01208 73118
www.borougharms.ukpub.net

DIRECTIONS:	see Getting to the start
PARKING:	30
OPEN:	daily; all day
FOOD:	daily
BREWERY/COMPANY:	Spirit Group
REAL ALE:	Sharp's Own and Doom Bar, Skinner's beers

(www.bodminandwenfordrailway.co.uk). Bodmin Gaol is a former country prison, built in 1778, with spooky underground passages where the Crown Jewels were stored during the First World War. There's plenty to keep children amused at Dobwalls Family Adventure Park, with stretches of miniature American railroads to ride, and action-packed areas filled with indoor and outdoor adventure play equipment (www.dobwallsadventurepark.co.uk).

A gentle ride along the banks of the St Austell River, with an optional extension to Heligan Gardens.

The Lost Gardens and Pentewan

Even if you don't get as far as the Lost Gardens of Heligan on your bike, you should somehow include it in your itinerary. Home of the Tremayne family for over 400 years, the story of the 'uncovering' of the gardens during the 1990s by Tim Smit (latterly of Eden Project fame) and his team is well known. But this is so much more than just a 'garden' – for a start it covers 200 acres – there's also a subtropical jungle, farm walks, fabulous vegetable gardens, various wildlife projects, and the romantic 'Lost Valley', as well as a farm shop, attractive restaurant, plants sales and shop.

It's worth taking some time to have a look around Pentewan village, with its narrow streets and attractive square. The glorious sandy beach, popular with holidaymakers, is featured in the Lloyds Bank 'Black Horse' advertisements. The old harbour opposite the Ship Inn is now silted up, a recurring problem during the life of the railway due to clay waste being washed downriver from the mines. This, and the growing importance of the ports at Par and Fowey, contributed to the closure of the Pentewan railway, which never reached the Cornwall Railway's main line, in 1918.

the ride

1 From the village car park return towards the B3273 and pass through the **parking area** for Pentewan Valley Cycle Hire, and round a staggered barrier onto the trail, which initially runs levelly through marshy woodland. The trail emerges from woodland onto the banks of the **St Austell River**, with a caravan site opposite.

2 Turn right and follow the trail along the riverbank. Watch out for pedestrians as this is a popular stretch. Along part of the trail walkers have the option of taking a narrow parallel route on a bank.

Top right: The Lost Gardens of Heligan
Left: Millennium signpost

3 Note the turn-off left across the river to the Lost Gardens of Heligan. Pass round the edge of a small parking area into **King's Wood** (owned by the Woodland Trust), and follow the trail as signed left back onto the riverbank. Dip into woodland again, then bear right, away from the river onto a **lane**, with a small parking area a little uphill to the right.

4 Turn left; pass a small parking area to meet a tarmac lane on a bend. Bear right as signed. Turn left opposite '**Brooklea**' and continue on a narrow wooded path, with a caravan site left. The track bears left at **Molingey** – with the London Apprentice on the other side of the river – then right to run along the right bank of the river again. Follow this tarmac way as it bears right through fields, then left along the edge of the **water treatment works**. Turn left for 50yds (46m) to meet the B3273. Turn right along the pavement.

5 Cross the lane to **Tregorrick**, and take the **second lane** on the left (Sawles Road – unsigned). Follow this quiet country lane to its end. For St Austell (and a possible extension to the Eden Project) turn left uphill to cross the A390. For Pentewan either turn around here, or for a more pleasant alternative, turn right and cycle steeply uphill through pleasant countryside. Drop to a T-junction and turn right, steeply downhill, through Tregorrick. On meeting the B3273 turn left to return to **Pentewan**.

6 **Heligan extension**: just after passing Point 2 above, turn right to cross the river on the **footbridge** (you must dismount). On reaching the B3273, turn left.

2h30	10 MILES	16.1 KM	LEVEL 2

SHORTER ALTERNATIVE ROUTE

1h30	7 MILES	11.3 KM	LEVEL 1

MAP: OS Explorer 105 Falmouth & Mevagissey

START/FINISH: Pentewan Valley Cycle Hire; grid ref: SX 017473

TRAILS/TRACKS: mainly well-surfaced track, some woodland paths, little roadwork

LANDSCAPE: woodland and fields, riverside, roadwork on extension

PUBLIC TOILETS: in centre of Pentewan

TOURIST INFORMATION: St Austell, tel 01726 879500

CYCLE HIRE: Pentewan Valley Cycle Hire, tel 01726 844242

THE PUB: The Ship, Pentewan

🚳 Busy roads (in season) and steep ascent/descent on Heligan extension

Getting to the start

Pentewan lies just off the B3273, about 1.5 miles (2.4km) north of Mevagissey. Lane-side parking in Pentewan is limited, but there is a free car park. Start at the cycle hire shop.

Why do this cycle ride?

This pleasant route, which opened in 1995, follows the line of the old Pentewan railway along the tranquil St Austell river. A loop through quiet lanes provides a convenient 'turnaround', and an optional, steep extension to the Lost Gardens of Heligan for those seeking more strenuous exercise.

Researched and written by: Sue Viccars

Pass the touring park left, then turn right to cross the road as signed. Turn left with the pavement, then continue on a track. This bears right, away from the road into **Tremayne Estate woodland**. Climb steadily uphill for 0.75 mile (1.2km), levelling off as the track passes beneath a road. Bear left to a fork; Mevagissey may be found via the right fork. Keep left to meet the road (note that this can be busy); turn left for 0.5 mile (0.8km) to find **Heligan** on the left.

7 On leaving Heligan, turn right along the road. Cycle gently downhill, with great views over St Austell Bay. Turn left on the **first narrow lane**, steeply downhill. On meeting the next minor road, turn left, even more steeply, to meet the B3273 opposite **Pentewan Sands Holiday Park**. Turn left towards the Esso garage, then right into Pentewan village.

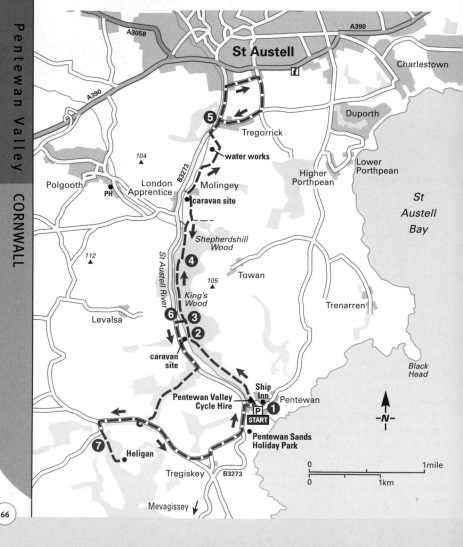

The Ship

about the pub

The Ship
West End, Pentewan
St Austell, Cornwall PL26 6BX
Tel: 01726 842855
www.staustellbrewery.co.uk

DIRECTIONS: see Getting to the start; pub on the main village street
PARKING: none
OPEN: daily; all day May to October
FOOD: daily
BREWERY/COMPANY: St Austell Brewery
REAL ALE: St Austell Tinner's Ale, Tribute and HSD

Festooned with colourful hanging baskets, the attractive Ship Inn fronts on to the main village street and is a real picture in summer, drawing in passing visitors, coast path walkers and cyclists fresh from the Pentewan Valley Trail. Tables fill early in the garden on fine days as they make the most of the pub's view across the village and the old harbour. The interior is equally appealing, with beams, shipwreck and maritime memorabilia, comfortable furnishings and a welcoming atmosphere filling the two bars, and there's the added attraction of the full complement of St Austell ales on hand-pump.

Food
Expect a traditional choice of pub meals that includes sandwiches, crusty baguettes, fisherman's lunch (smoked mackerel), steak and kidney pudding, and ham, egg and chips at lunch. Evening additions take in various grills and fresh local fish.

Family facilities
Children are allowed in the lounge bar where under 11s have a children's menu to choose from. Food is not served outside due to pestering crows and seagulls.

Alternative refreshment stops
There are cafés at the Lost Gardens of Heligan and a choice of pubs and cafés in Pentewan.

☛ Where to go from here
For an unforgettable experience in a breathtaking location, visit the Eden Project (www.edenproject.com) north of St Austell. It is the gateway into a fascinating world of plants and human society – space age technology meets the lost world in the biggest greenhouse ever built. There are two gigantic geodesic conservatories: the Humid Tropics Biome and the Warm Temperate Biome. To view the largest display of shipwreck artefacts in Britain, head for the Charlestown Shipwreck and Heritage Centre (www.shipwreckcharlestown.com), and for more information on the Lost Gardens of Heligan visit www.heligan.com.

From Fowey to Polkerris

Exploring the coast and countryside near Fowey where the writer Daphne du Maurier found inspiration for her romantic novels.

Daphne Du Maurier

Fowey and its environs inspired the writer Daphne du Maurier, who for many years lived as a favoured tenant at Menabilly House, the ancestral home of the Rashleigh family. The area became embedded in her work. Menabilly was the inspiration for the fictional house of 'Manderley' in du Maurier's *Rebecca*. The house also inspired the setting for *My Cousin Rachel*.

The walk starts from the charmingly named Readymoney Cove, a corrupted form of the Cornish 'redeman', possibly translating as 'stony ford'. From the cove you follow Love Lane, a very old cartway that rises over scarred rock slabs into the shrouding trees of Covington Wood. Soon open fields are reached and the route strikes inland along field paths and enclosed tracks. In the little valley below Lankelly Farm the path passes through a tunnel and beneath what was once a carriageway leading to Menabilly House. Beyond Tregaminion Farm and church the long western flank of the Gribbin Peninsula is reached. Here you divert down a zig-zag path to Polkerris Cove and beach.

Back at the church you head south to Polridmouth Cove ('P'ridmouth' to the initiated) and the heart of 'du Maurier Country'. From here you have a good view of Gribbin Head and its crowning 'Daymark', an immense edifice erected in 1832 as a warning mark to sailors.

The Daymark was erected on land granted by William Rashleigh of Menabilly. The inscription defines the mercantile priorities of the day, 'safety of commerce' first, 'preservation of mariners' second. From Polridmouth Cove a roller coaster hike takes you to St Catherine's Point and to the ruins of St Catherine's Castle. From the high ground of St Catherine's Point there is a steep descent to Readymoney Cove.

the walk

1 From the bottom end of the car park walk down St Catherine's Parade, then turn right towards the inlet of **Readymoney Cove**. Continue to the end of the road, above the beach and follow the initially rocky Love Lane uphill on the **Saints Way**. Carry on past the first junction, ignoring the options by a National Trust sign for 'Covington Woods'.

2 Turn left at the next junction and climb wooden steps to reach **Allday's Fields**. Follow the right-hand field edge. At a field gap follow an obvious grassy track ahead, crossing a stile by a gate to reach a lane end at **Coombe Farm**. Follow the lane ahead.

3 At a road, turn right and continue to **Lankelly Farm**. Pass a junction on the right and follow Prickly Post Lane for a few paces. Turn off left onto a **gravel drive**, then keep left and along a narrow fenced-in path.

4 Follow the path to the right of a house at **Trenant**, then cross the tarmac drive and the wall stile ahead. Keep ahead alongside the field edge, then steeply descend to a footbridge and a stile into a

Washing rocks as seen from St Catherine's Castle, Fowey

| 3h00 | 5 MILES | 8 KM | LEVEL 1 2 3 |

MAP: OS Explorer 107 St Austell & Liskeard

START/FINISH: Readymoney Cove car park, reached by continuing on from entrance to Fowey's main car park; grid ref: SX 118511

PATHS: field paths, rough lanes and coastal footpath, 8 stiles

LANDSCAPE: coastal fields, woodland and open coastal cliffs

PUBLIC TOILETS: Readymoney Cove and Polkerris

TOURIST INFORMATION: Fowey, tel 01726 833616

THE PUB: Rashleigh Inn, Polkerris

🅛 There are some steep ascents and descents on the coast path and paths can be muddy and slippery during wet weather. A walk for older, fitter family groups

Getting to the start

From the A390 east of St Austell take the A3082 through Par to reach Fowey. On the edge of the town follow signs for the Main Car Park, then continue (well-signed) to Readymoney Cove car park.

Researched and written by:
David Hancock, Des Hannigan

field below **Tregaminion Farm**. Go up the field to a gate, continue between buildings then turn right, then left, to reach a T-junction with a road by the entrance gate to the **little church** of Tregaminion.

5 Turn right and in 100yds (91m) go left into a field. Reach a junction on the edge of some woods and take the right-hand branch that zig-zags down to the beach, cove and Rashleigh Inn at **Polkerris**.

6 Retrace steps back up the zig-zag path and walk back to the church. Continue along the road to reach a car park, then proceed along the surfaced road, signposted **'Menabilly Farm'**. Continue when the surfaced road becomes a track and then a path, that descends to **Polridmouth Cove**. Turn left along the coast path.

7 Follow the coast path, signposted **'Lankelly Cliff'**. At open ground, follow the seaward field edge. Go steeply in to, and out of, Coombe Haven. Enter **Covington Wood**, keep left at the immediate junction.

8 Turn right at a junction to reach **St Catherine's Castle**. Return along the path then go down steps at the first junction on the right. Go down wooden steps to **Readymoney Beach**. Return to the car park via **St Catherine's Parade**.

what to look for

Along the vegetated borders of the fields and woods look for the tall, pinkish flower spike of rosebay willowherb. This tall plant with its purple flowers, which give way to cottony seeds in autumn, was once rare in Britain. It is thought that it spread rapidly throughout the country with the coming of the railways in the 19th century. The frequent scorching of embankments from stray sparks during the old days of steam trains created ideal growing conditions for the willowherb's windblown seeds. The web of railway lines also served as a disseminator for many other plants. Look for the madly tangled and trailing blooms of great bindweed, with their white flowerheads.

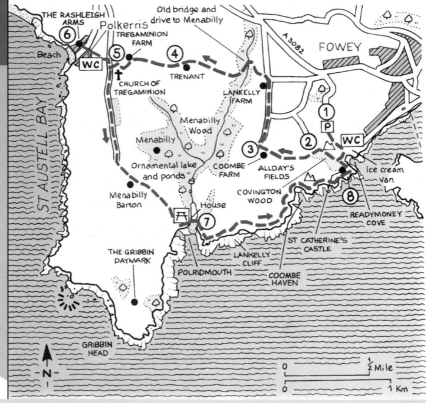

Rashleigh Inn

Literally on the beach in a tiny isolated cove and known locally as the 'Inn on the Beach', the Rashleigh is well worth seeking out for its magnificent setting. Once the lifeboat station before becoming a pub in 1924, it is a popular refreshment spot for coast path walkers and for families using the beach in the summer. Summer alfresco drinking is unrivalled in the area, for the table-filled terrace is a splendid place from which to watch the sun set across St Austell Bay. On cooler days the sea views can still be admired from the warmth of the main bar, especially from the bay-window seats.

Food

Bar food ranges from sandwiches, notably the Rashleigh Special – an open sandwich topped with crab and salad – to ploughman's lunches, fish pie, beer battered cod and chips, cottage pie, and daily fish specials. Separate restaurant menu.

Family facilities

Children are welcome inside the pub. Expect to find a children's menu, the availability of smaller portions, a high chair, baby-changing facilities, and reading books. Parents enjoying a drink on the terrace can keep an eagle eye on their children playing on the beach.

Alternative refreshment stops

There is usually an ice cream van at Readymoney Cove during the summer. The Lifeboat House café, opposite the Rashleigh Inn, offers coffee, tea and light lunches.

☛ Where to go from here

Visit the small and unspoilt village of Charlestown near St Austell, which has a unique sea lock and china clay port, purpose-built in the 18th century. The Shipwreck and Heritage Centre houses the largest display of shipwreck artefacts in the country, along with local heritage and diving exhibits (www.shipwreck-charlestown.com). At Wheal Martyn, north of St Austell, you can explore the China Clay Museum. The open-air site includes a complete 19th-century clayworks, with huge granite-walled settling tanks and working water wheels (www.wheal-martyn.com).

about the pub

Rashleigh Inn
Polkerris, Fowey
Cornwall PL24 2TL
Tel 01726 813991
www.rashleighinnpolkerris.co.uk

DIRECTIONS: village signposted off the A3082 between Fowey and St Austell; pub beside the beach

PARKING: 22

OPEN: daily; all day

FOOD: daily; all day

BREWERY/COMPANY: free house

REAL ALE: Sharp's Doom Bar, Timothy Taylor Landlord, Rashleigh Bitter, Cotleigh Tawny, guest beer

DOGS: not allowed inside

A coastal walk near Polruan

WALK

A woodland and coastal walk from the village of Polruan through the ancient parish of Lanteglos.

Old Cornwall

Parts of Cornwall are so encompassed by the sea that they seem genuinely out of this modern world. The sea is still their major highway. Polruan on the estuary of the River Fowey is one such place. The headland on which it stands has the sea on its southern shore and is bounded to the north by the calm and tree-lined tidal creek of Pont Pill.

The village can be reached by land only along minor roads, yet Polruan lies only a few hundred yards across the estuary from bustling Fowey and a regular passenger ferry runs between the two.

Polruan and its parish of Lanteglos are redolent of old Cornwall. Prehistoric settlers found a refuge on the narrow headland on which it stands, medieval worshippers set up chantries and chapels and merchants prospered from the sea trade into Fowey's harbour. During the wars of the 14th and 15th centuries, Fowey ships harried foreign vessels and earned themselves the sobriquet of 'Fowey Gallants'. The entrance

Polruan   CORNWALL

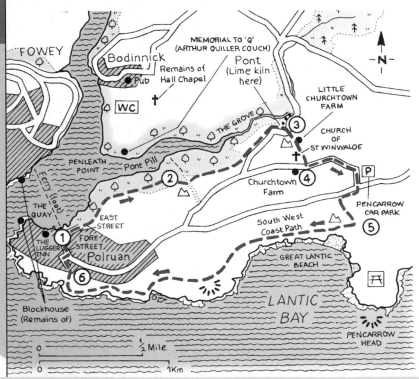

2h30 · 4 MILES · 6.4 KM · LEVEL 2

to the estuary was protected by a chain barrier. In peacetime the Gallants continued to raid shipping until Edward IV responded to complaints from foreign and English merchants by confiscating ships and removing the protective chain. The seamen then turned their hands successfully to fishing and smuggling.

The walk starts from Polruan and wanders through countryside that was once owned by medieval families who played a major part in the freebooting activities of Polruan seamen. Fortunes made through piracy were turned to legitimate trade and to farming and land management. The delightful countryside here is the product of long term land ownership and rural trade. At its heart lies the splendid Lanteglos Church of St Winwaloe, or St Willow. The second part of the walk leads back to the sea, to the steep headland of Pencarrow and to the dramatic amphitheatre of Lantic Bay. From here, the coastal footpath leads airily back to Polruan and to the rattle and hum of an estuary that has never ceased to be alive with seagoing.

the walk

1 Walk up from **The Quay** at Polruan, then turn left along East Street, by a **telephone box** and a seat. Go right, up steps, signposted 'To the Hills' and 'Hall Walk'. Go left at the next junction, then keep along the path ahead. Keep right at a junction and pass a National Trust sign, '**North Downs**'.

2 Turn right at a T-junction with a metalled track, then in just a few paces, bear off left along a path, signposted '**Pont and Bodinnick**'. Reach a wooden gate onto

---

MAP: OS Explorer 107 St Austell & Liskeard

START/FINISH: Polruan – parking on The Quay; grid ref: SX 126511. An alternative start to the walk can be made from the National Trust Pencarrow car park (Point 4, SX 149513). You can also park at Fowey's Central car park, then catch the ferry to Polruan

PATHS: good throughout, can be very muddy in woodland areas during wet weather, 3 stiles

LANDSCAPE: deep woodland alongside tidal creek and open coastal cliffs

PUBLIC TOILETS: Polruan

TOURIST INFORMATION: Fowey, tel 01726 833616

THE PUB: Lugger Inn, Polruan

⚠ One steep descent on exposed coast path

Getting to the start

Polruan can be reached via narrow lanes from Polperro and the A390 at Lostwithiel, via Lerryn and Penpoll. Alternatively, take the vehicle ferry from Fowey to Bodinnick, or park in Fowey (on the A3082 east of St Austell) and take the passenger ferry across the estuary to Polruan. Pay-and-display parking on The Quay in Polruan.

Researched and written by: David Hancock, Des Hannigan

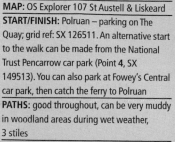

Stunning views from the South West Coast Path

a lane. Don't go through the gate, but instead bear left and go through a small gate. Follow a path, established by the National Trust, and eventually descend **steep wooden steps**.

3 At a T-junction with a track, turn right and climb uphill. It's worth diverting left at the T-junction to visit **Pont**. Reach a lane, go left for a few paces then, on a bend

by **Little Churchtown Farm**, bear off right through a gate signed 'Footpath to Church'. Climb steadily to reach the **Church of St Winwaloe** (pictured on page 73).

4 Turn left outside the church and follow a narrow lane. At a T-junction, just beyond **Pencarrow car park**, cross the road and go through a gate, then turn right along the field edge on a path established by the National Trust, to go through another gate. Turn left along the field edge.

5 At the field corner, turn right onto the coast path and descend very steeply. (To continue to Pencarrow Head go left over the stile here and follow the path onto the headland. From here the coast path can be re-joined and access made to Great Lantic Beach.) Follow the coast path for about 1.25 miles (2km), keeping to the cliff edge ignoring any junctions.

6 Where the cliff path ends, go through a gate to a road junction. Cross the road then go down **School Lane**. Turn right at Speakers Corner, then turn left down Fore Street to reach **The Quay** at Polruan.

what to look for

Spend some time exploring Polruan, at the beginning or end of the walk. This fine little port has retained much of its vernacular character in spite of some modern development. Polruan thrived because of seagoing and there is still a rich sense of those sea-dominated days in the narrow alleyways of the village.

The handsome Church of St Winwaloe, or St Willow, has notable wagon roofs containing some original 14th-century timbers as well as many other beams added during later centuries. The side walls and piers lean engagingly to either side. The novelist Daphne du Maurier was married here in 1932 and the church features as 'Lanoc Church' in her book The Loving Spirit.

Lugger Inn

Right beside The Quay and convenient for the passenger ferry to Fowey, this unassuming waterside pub enjoys super estuary views, especially from the family room. Down in the beamed bar traditional features include stone walls, a wood-block floor, high-backed settles, open fires, big model boats and photographs of the pub and village in days gone by. Locals congregate here or in the adjoining games room (pool table, TV) for pints of St Austell ales, and the pub is popular with diners for local fish and home-made pies.

Food

Menus take in traditional pub favourites and a good range of home-made dishes, such as chicken and ham pie, lasagne, fish crumble, vegetable curry and moussaka. Local fish includes freshly battered cod, sea bass and plaice. Soup and sandwiches are available at lunchtimes.

Family facilities

Families are welcome in the no-smoking restaurant area and there's a children's menu for smaller appetites.

about the pub

Lugger Inn
The Quay, Polruan, Fowey
Cornwall PL23 1PA
Tel 01726 870007

DIRECTIONS: see Getting to the start; pub beside The Quay

PARKING: public car park adjacent

OPEN: daily; all day

FOOD: daily

BREWERY/COMPANY: St Austell Brewery

REAL ALE: St Austell Tinner's Ale, Tribute and HSD (summer only)

DOGS: allowed in the bar area only

Alternative refreshment stops

There are a number of cafés and restaurants in Polruan and the Russell Inn is at the bottom of Fore Street.

☞ Where to go from here

Take the ferry over (or back to) Fowey and explore the narrow streets and visit St Catherine's Castle, a small 16th-century fort built by Henry VIII to defend Fowey Harbour (www.english-heritage.org.uk). Lanreath Farm and Folk Museum is a hands-on countryside museum reflecting bygone times in Cornwall. Implements and equipment from the farmhouse, dairy and farmyard are displayed. Visit Lanhydrock House, a magnificent late Victorian country house set in a superb parkland setting in the Fowey Valley. There are over 50 rooms to explore and large formal and woodland gardens to stroll around (www.nationaltrust.org.uk).

A coastal route from Crackington Haven

A coastal and inland walk with views of the spectacular north Cornish coast.

Crackington's cliffs

Crackington Haven has given its name to a geological phenomenon, the Crackington Formation, a fractured shale that has been shaped into contorted forms. On the sheared-off cliff faces, you can see the great swirls and folds of this sedimentary rock that was 'metamorphosised' by volcanic heat and contorted by geological storms of millions of years ago. The name Crackington derives from the Cornish word for sandstone, crak.

During the 18th and 19th centuries, Crackington Haven was a small port, landing coal and limestone, and shipping out local agricultural produce and slate. Plans to expand Crackington into a major port were made in the 19th century. The scheme did not materialise, otherwise the Crackington Haven of today might have been a dramatically different place.

Along the open cliff south from Crackington, the remarkable geology unfolds. Looking back from Bray's Point, you see the massive contortions in the high cliff face of Pencannow Point on the north side of Crackington. Soon the path leads above Tremoutha Haven and up to the cliff edge beyond the domed headland of Cambeak. From here there is a breathtaking view of the folded strata and quartzite bands of Cambeak's cliffs. A path leads out to the tip, but it is precarious and is not recommended.

A short distance further on you arrive above Strangles Beach where again you look back to such fantastic features as Northern Door. Where the route of the walk turns inland there are low cliffs set back

Left: Crackington Haven
Below: The headland beyond Strangles beach

from the main cliff edge. These represent the old wounds of a land slip where the cliff has slumped towards the sea. From here the second part of the walk turns inland and descends into East Wood and the peaceful Trevigue Valley, once a 'fjord' filled by the sea. Today much of the valley is a nature reserve and wandering down its leafy length is an antidote to the coastal drama of the Crackington cliffs.

the walk

1 From the Crackington Haven car park entrance go left across a bridge, then turn right at a **telephone kiosk**. Follow a broad track round to the left, between a signpost and an old wooden seat, then go through a kissing gate onto the coast path. At a fork follow the coast path right, signed '**Cambeak**'.

2 Cross a footbridge then, at a fork of paths, follow white arrow left and a path up a sheltered valley on the inland side of the steep hill. Continue on the **cliff path**.

3 Where a stretch of low inland cliffs begins, at a junction of paths and marker post, go left (signed '**Trevigue**') following the path to reach a road by a National Trust sign for **The Strangles**.

4 Go left, walking past the farm entrance to Trevigue, then, in just a few paces, turn right down a drive by the **Trevigue sign**. Then bear off to the left across the grass to go through a gate by a signpost.

| 1h45 | 3.5 MILES | 5.7 KM | LEVEL 2 |

MAP: OS Explorer 111 Bude, Boscastle & Tintagel

START/FINISH: Crackington Haven car park (can be busy in summer) or Burden Trust car park, along B3263 road to Wainhouse; grid ref: SX 145968

PATHS: good coastal footpath and woodland tracks, can be very wet and muddy, 9 stiles

LANDSCAPE: open coast and wooded valley

PUBLIC TOILETS: Crackington Haven

TOURIST INFORMATION: Bude, tel 01288 354240

THE PUB: Coombe Barton Inn, Crackington Haven

🛈 Coast path is steep in places and close to the cliff edge

Getting to the start

Crackington Haven is signposted off the A39 Bude to Wadebridge road at Wainhouse Corner, 7 miles (11.3km) south of Bude. It can also be reached from the B3263 north of Boscastle.

Researched and written by:
David Hancock, Des Hannigan

5 Go directly down the field, keeping left of a **telegraph pole**, to reach a stile. Continue downhill to the edge of a wood. Go down a tree-shaded path to a junction of paths in a shady dell by the river.

6 Turn sharp left here, following the signpost towards **Haven**, and continue on the obvious path down the wooded river valley.

7 Cross a footbridge, then turn left at a junction with a track. Cross another **footbridge** and continue to a gate by some houses. Follow a track and then a surfaced lane to the main road, then turn left to the **car park**.

what to look for

The field and woodland section of this walk supports a very different flora to that found on the heathery, windswept cliffland. Some of the most profuse fieldedge and woodland plants belong to the carrot family, the Umbelliferae. They may seem hard to distinguish, but the commonest is cow parsley, identifiable by its reddish stalk, feathery leaves and clustered white flower heads. Hogweed is a much larger umbellifer often standing head and shoulders above surrounding plants; it has hairy stalks and broad toothed leaves and can cause an unpleasant rash if it comes in contact with your skin. A third common umbellifer is the alexander, prolific in spring and early summer. It has broad, lime green leaves and clustered yellow florets.

Coombe Barton Inn

about the pub

Coombe Barton Inn
Crackington Haven, Bude
Cornwall EX23 oJG
Tel 01840 230345
www.combebartoninn.com

DIRECTIONS: see Getting to the start; pub beside car park	
PARKING: 25	
OPEN: daily; all day in summer	
FOOD: daily	
BREWERY/COMPANY: free house	
REAL ALE: St Austell Dartmoor Best and HSD, Sharp's Doom Bar	
DOGS: allowed in the bar	
ROOMS: 6 bedrooms, 3 en suite	

Originally built for the 'Captain' of the local slate quarry, the Coombe Barton (it means 'valley farm' in Cornish) is over 200 years old and sits In a small cove, opposite the beach and surrounded by spectacular rock formations. Much extended and modernised, it features a big, open-plan bar with local pictures on the walls and a surfboard hanging from the wood-planked ceiling – the pub is very popular with surfers from the beach. There's a screened off games area, a huge family dining area, and a summer terrace for alfresco eating and drinking. Bedrooms are comfortable and one suite is suitable for families.

Food

Local seafood is a feature of the menu and includes sea bass, lemon sole, plaice and halibut. Good range of daily specials, lunchtime sandwiches (try the local crab), vegetarian meals and Sunday roast carvery lunches.

Family facilities

Very popular with families seeking refreshment away from the beach, the pub welcomes children and offers a family dining area, high chairs, a children's menu and smaller portions.

Alternative refreshment stops

There are two cafés either side of the car park in Crackington Haven.

☛ Where to go from here

Head down the coast to Tintagel and explore the ruins of Tintagel Castle, one of the most spectacular spots in the country associated with King Arthur and Merlin (www.english-heritage.org). On the way, visit the renowned and attractive National Trust fishing village of Boscastle with its narrow, cliff-hung harbour entrance, small quay, Heritage Coast Visitor Centre, and walks through the beautiful Valency Valley and St Nectan's Glen.

Along Bude Bay

A pleasant stroll through coastal heathland where the cliff edges provide a refuge for masses of wild flowers.

Coastal flora and fauna

The windswept coastal grasslands of North Cornwall seem unlikely havens for plant life, but, around Bude, the cliff edges especially, provide a unique refuge for wild flowers. This walk follows the flat cliff land north of Bude with an inland section on the return. Along the way you'll find numerous wild flowers that turn the cliff top into a riot of colour in spring and early summer.

The walk starts from the northern outskirts of Bude at Crooklets Beach and quickly you're on cropped grasslands of the National Trust's Maer Cliff and Maer Down. In spring the dominant flower here is the spring squill. Other early plants which flourish here are the lilac-coloured early scurvy grass, the pink thrift and white sea-campion. At Northcott Mouth the cliffs give way to a wide stony beach. Here the route of the walk turns inland and climbs uphill to follow the line of an old bridleway, often choked with grass and brambles, but with typical hedgerow plants such as foxglove and red valerian poking through.

Soon you reach the road to Sandy Mouth Beach and the cliff path back to Crooklets. Once more there are many wild flowers here. The grass is laced with the yellow and orange flowers of kidney vetch and the yellow heads of hawkweed and, by July, is scattered with the pink and white florets of the aromatic wild carrot. From Crooklets the walk angles inland to a final stroll through an area of typically dense woodland, a dramatic

contrast in habitat to the open cliff top. Here primroses and daffodils appear in early spring. Sycamore, beech, alder, cypress, Scots pine and Corsican pine create a sheltered and moist environment within which plants like the tall yellow flag iris and the lilac-coloured water mint thrive.

The last section of the walk leads you past the Maer Lake Nature Reserve, which is flooded in winter. There is no public access to the area from the roadside but you can get an excellent view of the many birds through binoculars.

the walk

1 Go towards the beach, cross a bridge and head for some steps. Pass in front of **beach huts**, then turn left along a stony track between walls. Go up some steps and onto the **coast path**, signed 'Maer Cliff'.

2 Go through a gate and along a track behind a white building, called **Northcott House**. Bear off to the left, by a

signpost, down a path to the sea at **Northcott Mouth beach**. From here, bear right along a track that will take you back inland, past a group of houses on the left, and continue uphill to pass some more houses.

3 Where the track bends round to the right, leave it and keep straight ahead to a gate. Keep outside the left edge of the overgrown **bridle path** ahead.

4 Reach a field gate and follow a track through fields. Keep left at a junction with another track, then continue to a T-junction with a public road. Turn left and walk down the road, with care, to **Sandy Mouth**.

5 Pass the National Trust **information kiosk** and descend towards the beach, then go left and uphill and follow the coast path back to Northcott Mouth beach, and a **red lifeguard hut** passed earlier.

Bude harbour on Cornwall's north coast

2h30 · **5 MILES** · **8 KM** · **LEVEL 1** 2 3

MAP: OS Explorer 111 Bude, Boscastle & Tintagel and 126 Clovelly & Hartland
START/FINISH: Crooklets Beach Car Park (pay-and-display); grid ref: SS 204071
PATHS: excellent throughout, grassy coast path, field path, metalled lanes
LANDSCAPE: coastal cliffs
PUBLIC TOILETS: Crooklets Beach and Sandy Mouth
TOURIST INFORMATION: Bude, tel 01288 354240
THE PUB: The Inn on the Green, Bude
⚠ Keep well back from the cliff edges

Getting to the start

Follow signs off the A39 for Bude. Go through the town centre and follow signs to Crooklets and Poughill. Turn left at Flexbury on the northern edge of Bude for Crooklets Beach. Large pay-and-display car park by the beach.

Researched and written by:
David Hancock, Des Hannigan

WALK

6 Follow the roadside path just past the lifeguard hut and retrace your steps to the **white bungalow** passed earlier. Go along the track behind the building and then keep ahead along a broad track along the edge of **three fields**.

7 At a field corner by a **footpath sign** go through the open gateway ahead then turn left and follow the field edge into a hedged-in path. Continue between trees to a lane by a house at **Rosemerrin**. Continue to a road.

8 Turn right along the road, with **Maer Lake Nature Reserve** down to your left. Cross at a junction with Maer Down Road, go left, then right, passing **The Inn on the Green**, and return to the car park.

what to look for

Butterflies that are likely to be seen along the cliffs in summer include the meadow brown, probably Britain's commonest butterfly, its name a perfect description of its dusky colour. Look also for the common blue, a small butterfly with an almost lilac tinge, and for the glamorous painted lady with its tawny-orange wings and black and white markings. The painted lady's main habitat is Southern Spain and North Africa from where large swarms often migrate north in April and May, finding no difficulty in crossings of the English Channel.

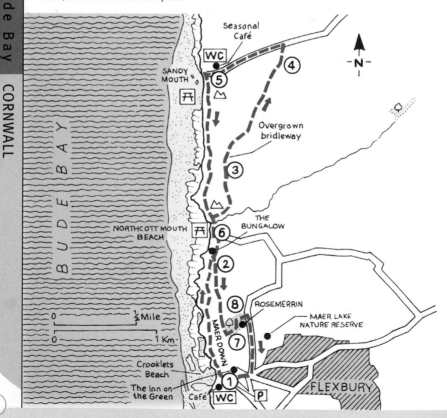

The Inn on the Green

Imposing, blue-painted inn/hotel built in 1900 and located just a stone's throw from Crooklets Beach and overlooking the broad expanse of Summerleaze Down and Bude golf course. Beyond the front summer terrace you will find a comfortable lounge bar furnished with sofas and easy chairs and decorated with beach-scene prints. The adjoining bar has chunky wooden tables and chairs and pool table.

Food

Lunchtime bar meals range from filled baguettes and sandwiches to ploughman's, beefburgers and jacket potatoes filled with chilli or tuna and mayonnaise. The more extensive evening menu includes pasta meals, fisherman's pie, beef stroganoff, pan-fried steaks with pepper, Stilton or mushroom sauce. Sunday roast lunches.

Family facilities

Children are welcome away from the bar and in the restaurant. There is a basic children's menu and smaller portions of the Sunday roast lunches are available.

Alternative refreshment stops

There is a National Trust seasonal café above Sandy Mouth Beach at the halfway point of the walk and there are a number of beachside cafés at Crooklets Beach.

☞ Where to go from here

Enjoy a drive north along the A39, visiting the village of Morwenstow, Cornwall's most northerly parish, along the way. The Church of St John Baptist contains the graves of over 40 shipwrecked sailors, buried by the eccentric Parson Hawker who spent 40 years here serving 'a mulititude of smugglers, wreckers and dissenters'. The church is fascinating and there are some beautiful clifftop views and walks. Venture further, into Devon, and you should visit Hartland Quay, once a thriving port for over 250 years before storms destroyed the harbour. The former harbour buildings comprise a hotel, shop and a small museum illustrating the history of this remarkable place.

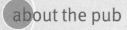

about the pub

The Inn on the Green

Crooklets Beach, Bude
Cornwall EX23 8NF
Tel 01288 356013
www.innonthegreen.info

DIRECTIONS:	see Getting to the start
PARKING:	Crooklets Beach Car Park
OPEN:	daily; all day
FOOD:	daily
BREWERY/COMPANY:	free house
REAL ALE:	Sharp's Doom Bar, St Austell Tinner's Ale
DOGS:	allowed in the bar
ROOMS:	26 bedrooms, 17 en suite

From Brownsham to Clovelly

Pheasants and follies – and a different way into Clovelly.

Clovelly

Clovelly is an extraordinary place, best seen early in the morning, or at the end of the day when it is quieter. Clinging to the wooded cliffs on the long, virtually uninhabited stretch of coastline between Bideford and Hartland Point, it has a timeless feel. Once famous as the village where donkeys carried goods and people up the perilously steep cobbled village street, today it is a tourist trap. Most people drive to the village and park at the Visitor Centre at the top, but it's much more satisfying to walk along the coast path from the National Trust lands at Brownsham. The two 17th-century farmhouses of Lower and Higher Brownsham, now holiday lets, lie just inland from one of the most unspoilt sections of the North Devon coastline.

Charles Kingsley, social reformer and author of *Westward Ho!* and *The Water Babies*, lived in Clovelly as a child when his father was rector there. Clovelly featured heavily in *Westward Ho!* (1855) when it came to the attention of the world. Up till then it had been reliant on herring fishing for its main source of income. Charles Dickens also mentioned Clovelly in *A Message from the Sea* (1860), so extending its new-found popularity.

Clovelly Court dates from around 1740, when the Hamlyns bought the Manor from the Carys, but was remodelled in Gothic style between 1790 and 1795. The gardens are open daily from 10am to 4pm. The much restored 15th-century All Saints Church has a Norman porch, dating from around 1300, and many monuments to the Cary and Hamlyn families. Sir James Hamlyn was responsible for the building of the Hobby Drive, which runs along the cliffs east of Clovelly, from which you get great views.

the walk

1 Leave the car park along the path nearly opposite the entrance. Walk alongside the field and through a gate into woods. Turn right, following signs '**footpath to coast path**' to pass a bench. Go straight on, signposted 'Mouth Mill & coast path'. Cross over a stile and on to meet the coast path.

2 Go right, over a stile into the field on **Brownsham Cliff**. There are good views ahead to **Morte Point**. Keep to the left edge, across a stile, down steps and left round the next field. Cross a stile and zig-zag downhill through woodland. When you leave the trees turn left towards the sea at **Mouth Mill**.

3 Follow the coast path across the stream by **stepping stones**. Clamber up the rocky gully left and turn right onto the **gritty track**, on a bend. Keep going left, uphill.

4 After 200yds (183m) follow **coast path signs** left, then immediately right. Go left up a narrow, wooded path uphill

18

WALK

Clovelly DEVON

| 2h45 | 5 MILES | 8 KM | LEVEL 1 2 3 |

MAP: OS Explorer 126 Clovelly & Hartland
START/FINISH: National Trust car park at Brownsham, grid ref: SS 285259
PATHS: grassy coast path, woodland and farm tracks, 5 dog-friendly stiles
LANDSCAPE: farmland, wooded coast path and deep combes
PUBLIC TOILETS: Clovelly Visitor Centre
TOURIST INFORMATION: Bideford, tel 01237 477676
THE PUB: The Red Lion, Clovelly
🛈 Undulating coast – some steep climbs

towards the cliffs below **Gallantry Bower**, with a 400ft (122m) drop into the sea.

5 Follow the signed path through woodland to pass the folly **'The Angel's Wings'**. Where a path leads straight on to the church, keep left following signs and via a gate through the edge of **Clovelly Court estate** (right). Pass into rhododendron woods via a kissing gate. The path winds down and up past a stone-built shelter, then through a kissing gate into a field. Keep to the left; through a series of kissing gates and oak trees to join the field again and meet the road at a **big gate**. Follow coast path signs across the road and on to the road that leads to the top of Clovelly village below the **visitor centre**.

6 Walk up deep, steep, ancient **Wrinkleberry Lane** (right of Hobby Drive ahead) to a lane, past the school and on to meet the road. Turn right; where the road bends right go through the gates to **Clovelly Court**. At the T-junction follow bridleway signs left (**'Court Farm & sawmills'**) through the farm, through a metal gate (sometimes open) and ahead along the track. Pass through a small wooded section and walk on to the hedge at the end of the field.

Getting to the start

From the A39 just west of Clovelly Cross roundabout, take the B3248 signed for Hartland. In a mile (1.6km) fork right towards Hartland lighthouse. Take the next right at Highdown Cross towards Brownsham. Fork right again, pass the National Trust buildings on the right and the car park is marked on the left.

Researched and written by:
Brian Pearse, Sue Viccars

7 Turn down to the right, then left though the hedge by a gate with a bridleway sign. At the bottom of the field go through a gate into a **plantation**, downhill.

8 Turn left at the forest track, following **bridleway signs**. Turn right up the long, gradually ascending track to **Lower Brownsham Farm**. Turn left up the road for the car park.

what to look for

Pheasants – and you don't have to look for them – you can't avoid them on this walk! You'll pass through much privately owned forestry, most of which is used for rearing pheasants. Britain's commonest game bird was introduced from Asia in the Middle Ages. The male is beautiful, with an iridescent green head and rich brown body. The female is smaller, duller and pale brown in colour.

Clovelly DEVON

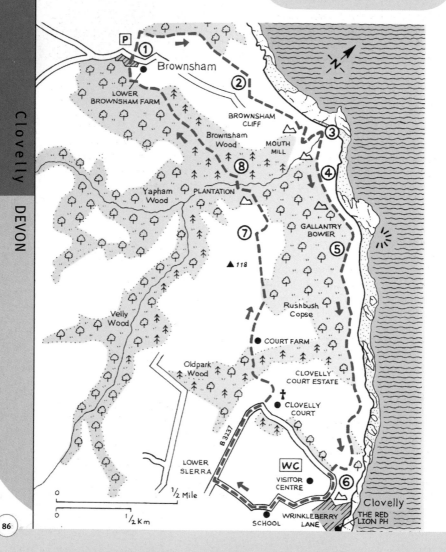

The Red Lion

Charming 18th-century hostelry situated right on the beach and the 14th-century harbour wall. Guests staying in the bedrooms can fall asleep to the sound of the sea on the shingle and wake up to wonderful views across Bideford Bay – it's a truly idyllic location. The main bar overlooks the quay and the old, original back bar, popular with locals, is mellow with age, comfortably furnished and has bare stone walls, a beamed ceiling, and an open fire burns in the grate on cold winter days.

Food
Seafood is a priority on the modern menu, which could include lobster salad, scallops with garlic butter, sea bass with hollandaise and cod and chips. Light lunchtime snacks are served in the bar.

Family facilities
Children of all ages are welcome at the Red Lion. There are two family bedrooms, a children's menu and high chairs for younger visitors, smaller portions from the main menu, and a designated family dining area.

Alternative refreshment stops
There are several pubs in Clovelly. At nearby Woolfardisworthy (Woolsery to the locals), there is the Farmer's Arms, the Manor Inn or fish and chips.

☛ Where to go from here
One of the West Country's leading family attractions (The Milky Way Adventure Park) is situated just 2 miles (3.2km) west of Clovelly. Attractions include Clone Zone, Europe's first interactive adventure ride featuring a suspended roller coaster.

There's also an indoor adventure play area, daily displays from birds of prey and a pets corner (www.themilkyway.co.uk). Visit the Big Sheep near Bideford, part of a large working sheep farm with sheep milking, shearing, feeding of lambs, sheepdog trials and hilarious sheep-racing (www.thebigsheep.co.uk)

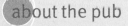

about the pub

The Red Lion
The Quay, Clovelly
Bideford, Devon EX39 5FF
Tel: 01237 431237
www.clovelly.co.uk

DIRECTIONS: see Getting to the start; a Land Rover service operates from the main village car park	
PARKING: use village car park	
OPEN: daily; all day	
FOOD: daily	
BREWERY/COMPANY: free house	
REAL ALE: Sharp's and Appledore beers	
DOGS: allowed in the bar	
ROOMS: 12 en suite	

The Tarka Trail – Braunton to Barnstaple

A gentle ride along the Taw estuary from historic Braunton to Barnstaple's old quayside.

Braunton Burrows

As you set off along the Tarka Trail from Braunton look right and in the distance you'll see a ridge of sand dunes (dating from the last Ice Age) – those nearest the sea are around 100ft (over 30m) high. This is Braunton Burrows, the second largest dune system in the UK, designated as an UNESCO International Biosphere Reserve in November 2002. The whole dune system is moving gradually inland, in some places as much as 10ft (3m) per year, and is well worth exploring. There are areas of managed meadowland, grassland, marsh and sandy habitats. Almost 500 different species of flowering plant have been identified, including 11 orchids. Sustainable tourism is the keyword here, and access for visitors is managed carefully so that fragile parts of the site are protected. The area is easily accessible by road or bike.

Braunton has a fascinating agricultural history, too. Between the village and the Burrows lies Braunton Great Field, a rare example of medieval strip farming. This area once lay beneath the sea and is extremely fertile. There's also an area of tidal saltmarsh, enclosed in the early 19th century for grazing cattle.

the ride

1 The car park marks the site of the old Braunton railway station, closed in 1965. The line – Barnstaple to Ilfracombe – was opened in 1874, and the last train ran in 1970. Cycle to the far end of the **car park** and turn right into the overflow area. Bear left and leave the car park by the police station (right). Bear right onto Station Road and cycle down it, passing the cycle hire on the left. Turn right into **Station Close** and then immediately left down a tarmac way. At the end cross the lane; keep ahead through black bollards to cross another lane, with a roundabout right.

On the Tarka Trail

1h30 — 11 MILES — 17.7 KM — LEVEL 1 23

2 Follow signs left to pick up the **old railway line**. Pass a wetland conservation area (left) and pass round a staggered barrier to cross a lane (the wire fences right mark the boundary of RAF Chivenor).

3 (Note: For The Williams Arms turn left here; at the end of the lane cross the A361 with care; the pub is on the other side.) Cycle on to reach a roundabout at the entrance to **RAF Chivenor**. The church ahead left is St Augustine's at Heanton Punchardon, built by Richard Punchardon (owner of Heanton estate) after his return from the Crusades in 1290. The village, formerly Heanton (Saxon Hantona – High Town) took on his name from that time. Cross the road by the roundabout and keep ahead through a wooded section.

4 Emerge suddenly from woodland onto the **Taw Estuary**, with far-reaching views. Listen for the oystercatcher's piping call, and watch out for curlew, easily identified by its curving bill. In winter thousands of migrant birds feed on the broad sandbanks here. Pass castellated **Heanton Court** on the left, a refuge for Royalists in the Civil War. The then owner of the Heanton estate, Colonel Albert Basset, fought for Barnstaple, which eventually fell to the Parliamentarians. Continue along the banks of the Taw to pass the **football club** (left).

5 Cross arched **Yeo Bridge**, a swing bridge over a tributary of the Taw, and pass the **Civic Centre** on the left (cyclists and pedestrians separate here). Bear left away from the river to meet the road. Turn right

MAP: OS Explorer 139 Bideford, Ilfracombe & Barnstaple

START/FINISH: Braunton car park (contributions), grid ref: SS 486365

TRAILS/TRACKS: level tarmac and gritty former railway track

LANDSCAPE: townscape, estuary

PUBLIC TOILETS: at start and in Barnstaple

TOURIST INFORMATION: Barnstaple, tel 01271 375000

CYCLE HIRE: Otter Cycle Hire, tel 01271 813339; Tarka Trail Cycle Hire, Barnstaple, tel 01271 324202

THE PUB: The Williams Arms, Wrafton

🛈 Busy crossing of A361 on route to the Williams Arms

Getting to the start

Braunton lies on the A361 Barnstaple to Ilfracombe road in north Devon. The car park is signed from the traffic lights in the centre of the village. If approaching from Barnstaple, turn left, and 100yds (91m) later turn left into the car park.

Why do this cycle ride?

Visiting Barnstaple by car at the height of the tourist season can be something of a trial as this north Devon market town, the oldest borough in the country, can get pretty choked by traffic. So what better way to get into the heart of Barnstaple than by cycling from Braunton via the Tarka Trail along the edge of the Taw estuary?

Researched and written by: Sue Viccars

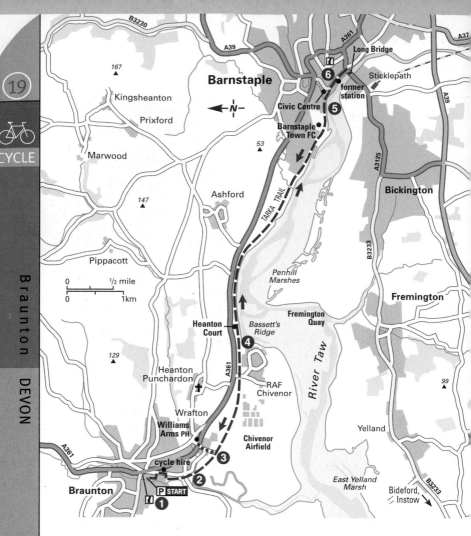

along the cycle path past **old Barnstaple Town Station** on the right (the railway reached the south side of the river in 1854, and this side in the early 1870s). Bear right as signed, then left along the **quay** (note: there is no wall along the edge).

6 Continue on to pass **Barnstaple Heritage Centre** (left), with its elaborate statue of Queen Anne. The Riverside Café (with cycle racks) lies a few yards along on the left, just before Barnstaple's Long Bridge over the Taw (there has been a bridge here since the 13th century). There is evidence of a settlement at Barnstaple from early Saxon times; trade via the Taw was vital to the town's prosperity for centuries. Queen Anne's Walk marks the site of the Great and Little Quays, once bustling with ocean-going ships, including five bound for Sir Francis Drake's Armada fleet in 1588.

The Williams Arms

A modernised thatched village pub that is well worth the short diversion off the trail as it is really geared up to family dining and has the added attractions of a play area and aviary in its spacious garden. Popular with both holidaymakers and locals, the two huge bars have been smartly refurbished with plush red carpets, a mix of modern furnishings and a self-service carvery, yet they retain some character in the form of low-beamed ceilings and open fires. Separate games area with pool table, darts and TV.

Food

The lounge bar menu offers a good choice of filled rolls and paninis, ploughman's lunches with home-cooked ham or local cheddar, steaks from the grill, and specialities like steak and venison pie, Exmoor venison braised in red wine and brandy, roast duck with orange sauce, and roast meats from the daily carvery

Family facilities

Children are welcome thoughout the pub. It is really geared to family dining and you'll find a games/TV room, a basic kid's menu, smaller portions for older children, high chairs, and a play fort and aviary in the large garden.

about the pub

The Williams Arms
Wrafton, Braunton
Devon EX33 2DE
Tel 01271 812360
www.williams-arms.co.uk

DIRECTIONS: the pub is beside the A361 Braunton to Barnstaple road, 1 mile (1.6km) south east of Braunton. See Point 3
PARKING: 100
OPEN: daily; all day
FOOD: daily
BREWERY/COMPANY: free house
REAL ALE: Bass

Alternative refreshment stops

There are plenty of pubs and cafés in Braunton and Barnstaple, and en route you'll find Heanton Court, another family-friendly pub.

➡ Where to go from here

On the edge of Exmoor at Blackmoor Gate is the Exmoor Zoological Park, which specializes in smaller animals, many endangered, such as the golden headed lion tamarins. There are contact pens and children are encouraged to participate (www.exmoorzoo.co.uk).
Combe Martin Wildlife Park and Dinosaur Park is a subtropical paradise with hundreds of birds and animals and animatronic dinosaurs, plus there are sea lion shows, falconry displays and animal handling sessions (www.dinosaur-park.com).

The Tarka Trail – Instow to Barnstaple

Fremington Quay

There's little evidence at Fremington Quay today to suggest that in the mid 19th century this was said to be the busiest port between Land's End and Bristol. The deepwater quay was built in the 1840s (with a horse-drawn rail link to Barnstaple), when silting of the River Taw prevented large ships from going further upriver. Before that time a local port operated from Fremington Pill, which the trail crosses en route for Fremington Quay. The main exports were clay and minerals, the main imports coal and limestone from south Wales for burning in local limekilns. The quay received another boost to its fortunes in 1854 when the main line railway reached Barnstaple, and lead to further development of the line to Bideford, which opened to passengers in late 1855. Exports of clay – from as far away as Peters Marland, 16 miles (25.7km) away – continued until the early 20th century.

The railway was closed in the 1960s, and the quay was taken out of use in 1969. Today the café and heritage centre, which opened in 2001, are housed in the reconstructed station building and signal box. There are picnic tables outside the café with lovely views across the Taw. The decline of shipping in the estuary, and the disappearance of local railways, has had a beneficial effect on local flora and fauna.

the ride

1 Turn left out of the car park and cycle along Marine Parade, passing **The Quay Inn** on the left. At the restored signal box (built in the early 1870s) turn left onto the **old railway line**.

2 The trail runs through a long cutting before emerging through an area of **wooden chalets**, with views left across dunes to the junction of the Torridge and Taw rivers, with the southern end of the sand dunes at Braunton Burrows beyond. Pass the **cricket ground** left, and then a picnic area and car park.

3 Continue over the access road to a **small industrial area** and then you're right out in the open. Pass East Yelland and Home Farm marshes and then the RSPB's **Isley Marsh reserve**, a saltmarsh habitat and high-tide roost. A short run through a wooded cutting leads to the viaduct over Fremington Pill – look left to see a lime kiln – and **Fremington Quay**.

4 The trail (now tarmac) passes in front of the café, then bears right past a parking and **picnic area** (left) and through a wooded cutting. A long embanked stretch leads all the way to Barnstaple. Penhill Marshes (jutting out into the estuary just east of Fremington Quay) have been reclaimed for grazing livestock. Along the trail you'll spot the 'creeps' – tunnels through the embankment enable cattle to access drier land at times of high tide. The large expanses of saltmarsh and mudflats along the estuary provide important habitats for a wide range of highly specialised plants and wildlife. Oystercatcher and redshank, among many other species, overwinter here. In late summer look out for the golden flowers of the sea aster, one of the few plants that can cope with being submerged by saltwater, and which helps to stabilise the marshes. In the cuttings either side of the Quay see if you can spot blue field

scabious in summer, and spotted meadow brown butterflies feeding on its flowers.

The trail narrows as the edge of **Sticklepath** (opposite Barnstaple) is reached: cyclists are asked to give way to pedestrians.

5 Where the road bridge (A3125) can be seen ahead, bear left for 20yds (18m). At the next junction bear left for the **Long Bridge** if you want to go into Barnstaple; if not, retrace your route to the cricket ground (see Point 2).

6 Just after the entrance to the ground, turn right on a narrow path as signed for the Wayfarer Inn and **beach café**. Meet a track running through the dunes and turn left, passing the café on the right. Emerge onto the road and keep ahead along the seafront, to find the car park on the left. This alternative return gives lovely views over **the Torridge** towards the attractive fishing village of Appledore, an important port in Elizabethan times. During the 18th century Bideford and Appledore were the largest importers of tobacco in the country; today Appledore is famous for its shipbuilding tradition. Much of the village's network of narrow streets and cobbled courtyards is a conservation area; catch the ferry from Instow Quay for a closer look.

2h30 — **13 MILES** **20.9 KM** **LEVEL 123**

MAP: OS Explorer 139 Bideford, Ilfracombe & Barnstaple

START/FINISH: Instow car park (fee-paying), grid ref: SS 472303

TRAILS/TRACKS: level tarmac and gritty former railway track

LANDSCAPE: townscape, estuary

PUBLIC TOILETS: Instow; Fremington Quay

TOURIST INFORMATION: Barnstaple, tel 01271 375000

CYCLE HIRE: Biketrail, Fremington Quay, tel 01271 372586; Bideford Cycle Hire, East-the-Water, tel 01237 424123

THE PUB: The Quay Inn, Instow

🛈 Fremington Quay very busy with bikes and people at peak holiday times

Getting to the start

Instow lies on the Torridge Estuary signed off the B3233 Barnstaple to Bideford road. Approaching from Barnstaple, take the second sign right. From Bideford, take the first sign left. Pass The Quay Inn on the right and the car park in about 100yds (91m).

Why do this cycle ride?

This second chunk of the Tarka Trail can be linked with either the route from Torrington to Bideford, or that from Braunton to Barnstaple. It stands on its own, however, as an easy ride from the delightful village of Instow along the southern side of the Taw Estuary to Barnstaple, passing historic Fremington Quay.

Researched and written by: Sue Viccars

20

CYCLE

Instow

DEVON

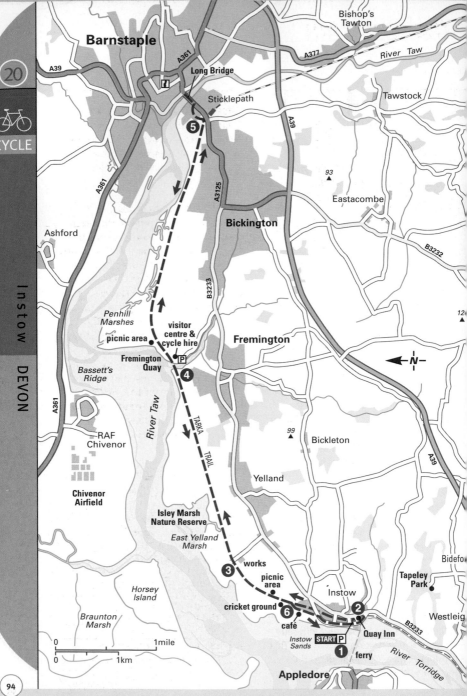

Instow DEVON

Barnstaple

Bishop's
Tawton

River Taw

A377

A361

Long Bridge

A39

Sticklepath

Tawstock

5

A3125

93

Eastacombe

Ashford

A361

Bickington

B3232

Penhill
Marshes

picnic area

visitor
centre &
cycle hire

B3233

Fremington

12

Fremington
Quay

4

Bassett's
Ridge

TARKA TRAIL

River Taw

A361

RAF
Chivenor

99

Bickleton

A39

Chivenor
Airfield

Isley Marsh
Nature Reserve

East Yelland
Marsh

Yelland

works

Bidefo

3

picnic
area

Tapeley
Park

Horsey
Island

cricket ground

6

Instow

Westleig

café

B3233

Braunton
Marsh

Instow
Sands

START P

1

Quay Inn

2

0   1mile
0   1km

ferry

River Torridge

Appledore

The Quay Inn

Lively and interesting little pub situated right on the quay with super views across the estuary from waterside tables outside the pub. The interior is rustic, open-plan and full of character, attracting a mixed clientele, from local fishermen and holidaymakers to walkers and cyclists on the Tarka Trail in search of refreshment. Locally brewed beers, perhaps Jollyboat ales from Bideford or Barum ales from Barnstaple, are particularly popular, as are the summer afternoon teas.

Food

The bar menu is huge, offering something for everyone, from crusty baguettes and crab salad to breaded plaice, fish pie, salmon and prawn fishcakes, and lamb shank with mash and rosemary gravy. Daily specials include fresh local fish like sea bass and plaice.

Family facilities

Although there is no specific family room children are welcome inside the pub. There are special meals for younger children and smaller portions are available.

Alternative refreshment stops

There are plenty of pubs, cafés and restaurant to choose from in Barnstaple. There's a café at the old station at Fremington Quay and the New Inn in Fremington.

☛ Where to go from here

Appeldore is home to the North Devon Maritime Museum where you can learn about the ship and boat building industry and the maritime activities of the area. Youngsters will love the Gnome Reserve and Wildflower Garden near Bradworthy (www.gnomereserve.co.uk), and the exhilarating rides and shows at the Milky Way Adventure Park near Clovelly (www.themilkyway.co.uk). Equally fascinating is the Quince Honey Farm at South Molton where you can follow the story of honey and beeswax from flower to table, as well as see the world of bees close up and in complete safety (www.quincehoney.co.uk).

about the pub

The Quay Inn

Marine Parade, Instow
Bideford, Devon EX39 4HY
Tel; 01271 860624

DIRECTIONS:	see Getting to the start
PARKING:	none
OPEN:	daily; all day
FOOD:	daily
BREWERY/COMPANY:	free house
REAL ALE:	changing local guest beers

The Tarka Trail – Great Torrington to Bideford

Tarka the Otter

The Tarka Trail is named after the hero of north Devon, author Henry Williamson's famous novel *Tarka the Otter*, published in 1927. Williamson moved to Georgeham, near Braunton in 1921, having visited the area in 1914, at which time he became captivated by this remote part of north Devon. He came here both to recover from the horrors of active service in World War One and also to write, and between 1921 and 1972 almost 50 works were published. His best known is the tale of Tarka the Otter, much of which is based around the River Torridge, which flows northwest for 9 miles (14.5km) from its source to its junction with the River Taw just beyond Appledore. Tarka

was born just below Canal Bridge, downstream from Torrington, and met his end on the River Torridge too. The story was made into a film and, by strange coincidence, Williamson died on the same day as the filming of Tarka's death scene, in 1977. It seems fitting that today, after many years of decline, otters are returning to Devon's rivers as a result of deliberate policy to improve habitat and water quality.

the ride

1 Turn right along the A386 and descend to pick up the Tarka Trail on the right before **Rolle Bridge**. It runs between The Puffing Billy – the old station building – and cycle hire in the goods yard opposite. Turn left along the trail to pass the pub and garden (cycle racks) on the left. The railway reached Bideford (from Barnstaple) in 1855; the extension (under the London and South Western Railway) from Bideford to Torrington opened July 1872, and closed in the mid 1960s. The 'Atlantic Coast Express' ran from here all the way to London Waterloo. Cycle over the **River Torridge** as it loops its way towards the sea.

2 Pause at the next river crossing to look at **Beam Weir**; as you cross the river for the third time look left towards Beam Aqueduct. Part of the railway utilised the bed of the former Rolle Canal, involved in a scheme to link with the Bude Canal in north Cornwall; only a 6-mile (9.7km) section was completed, in 1827. Lime and coal were carried inland from the coast to Torrington,

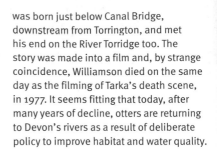

A fisherman on the River Torridge where Henry Williamson set his novel Tarka the Otter

and agricultural produce exported. Pass a **picnic area** left, and continue between the A386 and the Torridge (right). Look right through the trees towards Weare Giffard, with its 14th-century church and 15th-century manor house. Pass **Weare Giffard Cross** (left).

3 Where the Torridge takes a wide loop east cycle through **Landcross Tunnel** (lit), then through a cutting by Landcross Bridge. Now with the River Yeo on the left, cycle on to meet the **old iron railway bridge** over the Torridge.

4 The whole feel of the route changes here: the river is wide and slow, with large expanses of saltmarsh and reedbed – home to sedge warbler and reed bunting – and beautiful views. The bridge overlooks the 'Pool of the Six Herons' (mentioned in *Tarka*) – look out for herons, lapwing, redshank and curlew. Saltmarsh plants (specially adapted to seawater inundations) and reedbeds protect the river banks from erosion, and the mudflats support millions of invertebrates, food for wading birds. Limestone was shipped in from south Wales for burning in the limekiln left of the bridge; local woodland supplied timber for charcoal.

5 Continue along the right bank of the Torridge, with increasingly good views of **Bideford**, a significant port in medieval times, today a busy market town and

2h30	11 MILES	17.7 KM	LEVEL 1

MAP: OS Explorer 126 Clovelly & Hartland
START/FINISH: car park on Great Torrington Common, grid ref: SS 485193
TRAILS/TRACKS: level former railway track, now smooth tarmac
LANDSCAPE: woodland, river and estuary, saltmarsh, townscape
PUBLIC TOILETS: near Bideford station
TOURIST INFORMATION: Bideford, tel 01237 477676
CYCLE HIRE: Torridge Cycle Hire, Station Yard, tel 01805 622633; Bideford Cycle Hire, East-the-Water, tel 01237 4241123
THE PUB: The Puffing Billy, Great Torrington

Getting to the start

From Great Torrington take the A386 Bideford road across Great Torrington Common. Use the car park on the common opposite the junction with the B3227.

Why do this cycle ride?

The Tarka Trail, a 180-mile (290km) cycleway and footpath, offers great opportunities for exploring north Devon. The trail opened in May 1992, and those sections along former railway lines make great cycling routes. This ride from Great Torrington to Bideford, along the broad banks of the River Torridge, is one of three options, and can easily be linked to the route from Instow to Barnstaple.

Researched and written by: Sue Viccars

working port. Its 24-arched stone bridge recalls the town's early prosperity – it is said that each arch was funded by a local parish, and the size of the arch reflects their respective wealth! The 19th-century novelist Charles Kingsley (who lived at Clovelly during his childhood) described Bideford as 'the Little White Town that slopes upward from its broad river tide': little has changed.

6 Turn around is **old Bideford Station** – 220.5 miles (355km) from Waterloo! The Tarka Trail goes on to Instow. Refreshments are available from the **Railway Carriage Visitor Centre**. If you have time when you finish the ride, take a look around Great Torrington, noted for the Battle of Great Torrington in 1646, the end of Royalist resistance in the West Country in the Civil War.

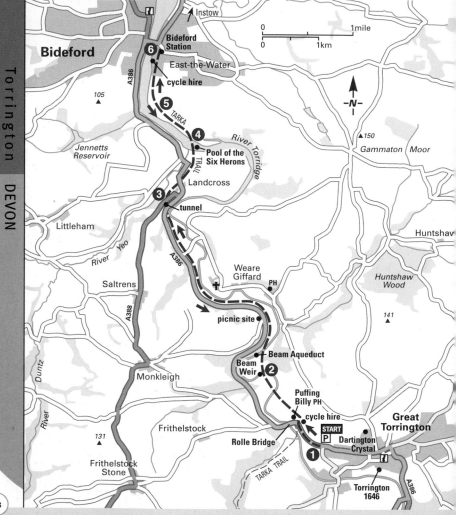

The Puffing Billy

Smack beside the former railway route and looking every inch the old station building it once was, the Puffing Billy is gradually being restored and makes the ideal post-ride refreshment stop on this section of the Tarka Trail. On fine days you can relax in the trail-side garden with a pint of locally-brewed Cavalier ale. There's a real sense of history inside due to the mass of authentic railway and station memorabilia that fills the atmospheric bars, including the original signs and platform notices used at the station.

Food

Call in during the morning for coffee, bacon sandwiches and croissants from the Early Morning Shunters menu. On the daytime menu you'll find baguettes and ploughman's lunches, ham, egg and chips and steak and kidney pie. Specials may take in lasagne, spaghetti carbonara and mixed grills, and a separate menu is served in the Station Restaurant.

Family facilities

The pub is very child friendly; they are welcome everywhere and there's a children's menu and a big play area outside in the garden.

Alternative refreshment stops

There's a good choice of pubs and cafés in Bideford, including at Bideford old station, your turn-around point.

☞ Where to go from here

Take a fascinating factory tour at Dartington Crystal in Great Torrington and watch craftsmen transform hot molten crystal into elegant glassware from the safety of elevated viewing galleries. Children can have fun in the glass activity area and you can discover the story of glass and the history of Dartington at the Visitor Centre (www.dartington.co.uk). Stroll down the steep cobbled street of Clovelly, one of Devon's most famous coastal villages, or visit the Milky Way Adventure Park to experience some exhilarating rides and shows (www.themilkyway.co.uk). Another family attraction – The Big Sheep (www.thebigsheep.co.uk) – is close to Bideford.

about the pub

The Puffing Billy
Station Hill, Great Torrington
Devon EX38 8JD
Tel 01805 623050

DIRECTIONS: right off the A386 1 mile (1.6km) west of Great Torrington, just before Rolle Bridge over the River Torridge

PARKING: 30

OPEN: daily; all day Easter to October; closed Wednesdays November to Easter

FOOD: daily

BREWERY/COMPANY: free house

REAL ALE: Clearwater Cavalier and 1646, guest beers

Calstock and Cotehele House

A stroll along the River Tamar from Calstock's Victorian viaduct to the Tudor manor house of Cotehele.

Calstock and Cotehele

The River Tamar seems to take its ease at Calstock and Cotehele, where it coils lazily through the lush countryside of the Devon/Cornwall border. Today all is rural peace and quiet. Yet a century ago Calstock was a bustling river port, and had been since Saxon times. Victorian copper and tin mining turned Calstock into an even busier port at which all manner of trades developed, including shipbuilding. The coming of the railway brought an end to Calstock's importance. The mighty rail viaduct of 1906, which spans the river here is an enduring memorial to progress and to later decline, yet the Calstock of today retains the compact charm of its steep riverside location. The viaduct was built from specially cast concrete blocks – 11,000 of them were made on the Devon shore – and it is a tribute to its design that such thoroughly industrial architecture should seem so elegant today and should have become such an acceptable element in the Tamar scene.

The area's finest architectural gem is the Tudor manor house of Cotehele, the focus of this walk. Cotehele dates mainly from the late 15th and early 16th centuries. In the 17th century the Edgcumbe family, who owned the estate, transferred their seat to Mount Edgcumbe House overlooking Plymouth Sound. Cotehele ceased to be the family's main home and the house was spared too much overt modernisation. Soon the Edgcumbes came to appreciate

the value of the house's Tudor integrity and Cotehele seems to have been preserved for its own sake, from the 18th century onwards.

The Edgcumbes gave the house to the National Trust in 1947 and Cotehele survives as one of the finest Tudor buildings in England. The medieval plan of the house is intact; the fascinating complex of rooms, unlit by artificial light, creates an authentic atmosphere that transcends any suggestion of 'theme park' history. This is a real insight into how wealthier people lived in Tudor Cornwall. Cotehele was built with privacy and even defence in mind and the materials used are splendidly rustic. The exterior façades have a rough patina that adds to the authenticity.

The early part of the walk leads beneath an arch of the Calstock Viaduct and on along the banks of the river, past residential properties where busy quays and shipbuilding yards once stood. Most of the walk leads through the deeply wooded Danescombe Valley, whose trees crowd round Cotehele in a seamless merging with the splendid estate gardens. The gardens support azaleas and rhododendrons and a profusion of broadleaf trees, the whole interspersed with terraces and such charming features as a lily pond, a medieval dovecote and a Victorian summerhouse. Below the house, at Cotehele Quay, the preserved sailing barge, the Shamrock, and the National Maritime Museum's exhibition rooms, commemorate the great days of Tamar trade. As you walk back to Calstock, along an old carriageway and through the deeper recesses of the Danescombe Valley, it is easy to imagine the remote, yet vibrant life of this once great estate and of the busy river that gave it substance.

the walk

1 From the car park walk to the left of the Tamar Inn, then turn left into **Commercial Road**. In a few paces take the second turning left and go along Lower Kelly Lane and beneath **Calstock Viaduct**.

2 In 0.5 mile (800m) keep left at a fork just past the large house with a veranda. Beyond a row of cottages, branch left, signposted **'Cotehele House'**, and follow a broad track uphill and beneath trees.

3 Go right at a junction, signposted 'Cotehele House'. Pass above a dovecote in **Cotehele Gardens**, then turn left at a T-junction. Go through a gate and turn right for the entrance to Cotehele House.

4 Follow the road from **Cotehele House**, then branch left and downhill to reach

Pretty Calstock with the viaduct in the background

| 2h00 | 4 MILES | 6.4 KM | LEVEL 1 23 |

MAP: OS Explorer 108 Lower Tamar Valley & Plymouth

START/FINISH: Calstock Quay free car park, grid ref: SX 436683

PATHS: excellent woodland tracks, can be muddy in places

LANDSCAPE: wooded riverside

PUBLIC TOILETS: Calstock Quay, Cotehele House, Cotehele Quay

TOURIST INFORMATION: Tavistock, tel 01822 612938

THE PUB: Tamar Inn, Calstock

Getting to the start

Calstock is 2 miles (3.2km) off the A390 midway between Tavistock and Callington, signposted at St Ann's Chapel. Follow signs in village to Quay and car park – limited spaces and often full by mid-morning.

Researched and written by:
David Hancock, Des Hannigan

WALK

Calstock

CORNWALL

Cotehele Quay. (You can continue from the Quay for just under 0.5 mile/800m to visit Cotehele Mill.)

5 Walk past the **Edgcumbe Arms Tea Rooms** towards the car park and follow a wooded path that starts beside the car park. Pass a little chapel and then a superb **viewpoint** to Calstock. At a junction, go right, signposted to **Calstock**. In a few paces branch left up a rising track.

6 Go right at a junction and descend to a wooden footbridge over a stream. At a T-junction with another track, turn left and walk up the track for about 55yds (50m).

7 Turn sharply right and go up a rising track along the side of a stone wall. Pass an **old well** on your left, then pass a junction with a track coming in from the left.

what to look for

The deep oak and beech woods that cloak the Danescombe Valley and Cotehele are a haven to wild life. The otter, an endangered species, may still be found along the Tamar's banks and although you would be immensely lucky to spot one, keep your eyes peeled. Buzzards lord it above clearings in the trees and above the neighbouring meadows. Along the minor streams, kingfishers patrol their territory, although again you need to keep a sharp lookout for them. In spring and early summer, the woods and meadows round Cotehele are thick with daffodils and bluebells.

8 Join the surfaced lane just before the big house with a veranda, passed earlier. Retrace your steps to **Calstock Quay**.

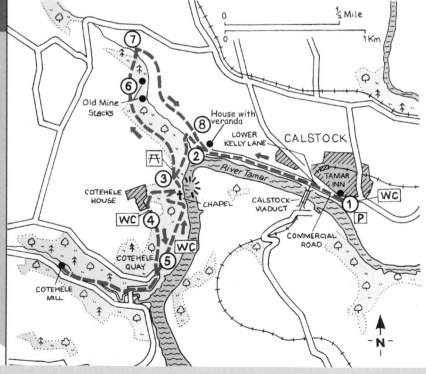

Tamar Inn

Just a stone's throw from the tidal Tamar, this large, 400-year-old inn was built as a hotel when Calstock was a busy and thriving port. Today it serves a loyal local trade and tourists and walkers exploring nearby Cotehele. There's a lively front bar where locals congregate to play pool and quaff locally brewed beers (tapped from the barrel). Beyond is a quieter bar area and a spacious dining area with access to a sun-trap decked terrace and views to the river.

Food

Bar food takes in light bites – Parma ham salad and sandwiches – sound favourites like steak and kidney pudding and venison sausages and mash, and fishy options, perhaps beer battered cod and Tamar fishpot medley.

Family facilities

Children are welcome in the pub. There's a kiddies section on the menu, smaller portions of main meals and Sunday roast lunches.

about the pub

Tamar Inn
The Quay, Calstock
Callington, Cornwall PL18 9QA
Tel: 01822 832487

DIRECTIONS: see Getting to the start; pub opposite the Quay

PARKING: use public car park opposite

OPEN: daily; all day

FOOD: no food Sunday evenings in winter

BREWERY/COMPANY: free house

REAL ALE: Sharps Doon Bar, Sutton Dartmoor Pride, guest beers

DOGS: allowed inside

Alternative refreshment stops

The Barn Restaurant is a National Trust restaurant within the Cotehele House complex. It serves morning coffee, afternoon tea and meals using local produce. The Edgcumbe Arms Tea Room is an attractive small restaurant at Cotehele Quay.

☞ Where to go from here

At Cotehele Quay allow time to visit the outstation of the National Maritime Museum, where the story of Tamar River trade throughout the centuries is told in old pictures and displays, and walk the extra 0.5 mile (800m) to see the restored Cotehele Mill (www.nationaltrust.org.uk). Visit Morwellham Quay near Gunnislake, once the greatest copper port in Queen Victoria's empire. You can ride by electric tramway underground into a copper mine. Staff wear Victorian costume and you can try on outfits in the Limeburner's Cottage.

Mount Edgcumbe Country Park

A walk round the Mount Edgcumbe estate on the shores of Plymouth Sound.

Mount Edgcumbe

The Mount Edgcumbe Country Park is a green oasis that flies in the face of Plymouth's crowded waterfront opposite. The two are separated by The Narrows, a few hundred yards of the 'Hamoaze', the estuary formed by the rivers Tavy, Lynher and Tamar. Mount Edgcumbe stands on the Cornish side of the river, although it was not always 'Cornish'. In Anglo Saxon times, Devon extended across the estuary as far as Kingsand. Today, however, Mount Edgcumbe and its waterfront settlement of Cremyll are emphatically Cornish. They stand on the most easterly extension of the Rame Peninsula, known with ironic pride by local people as the 'Forgotten Corner'. In truth Rame is one of the loveliest parts of the South West, let alone of Cornwall, and this walk takes you round the shores of the inner estuary, and then over the spine of the eastern peninsula, before returning to Cremyll along the open of Plymouth Sound.

The first section of the route takes you to peaceful Empacombe, where there is a tiny harbour contained within a crescent-shaped quay. It was here, during 1706-9, that workshops servicing the building of the famous Eddystone Lighthouse were located. Behind the

harbour is the Gothic façade of Empacombe House.

The path follows the wooded shoreline of the tidal basin known as Millbrook Lake, then climbs steeply inland to reach Maker Church on the highest point of the peninsula, with views up the Tamar to the Saltash bridges. From here you wander through tiny fields to reach a track that descends to the coast path on the southern side of the peninsula and the more bracing sea shore of Plymouth Sound. Finally you reach the delightful park environment that surrounds Mount Edgcumbe House where you can explore the lovely gardens.

the walk

1 From the car park go left along the footway opposite the entrance. Where the footway ends at an **old fountain** and horse trough, cross back left and go through a gap by a telephone kiosk, signposted '**Empacombe**'. Alternatively, from the ferry slipway, turn left to the old fountain, then cross to the right. Keep left past the **Old School Rooms**. Turn right at a junction then pass an obelisk and follow the path alongside the tree-hidden creek to Empacombe.

2 At a surfaced lane, by a house, keep ahead and go down to **Empacombe Quay**. Turn left beyond the low wall (dogs under control please) and skirt the edge of the small harbour to reach a stone stile onto a wooded path. Continue round **Palmer Point** and on to a public road.

The folly (left) and gardens (above) in Mount Edgcumbe Country Park

| 3h00 | 6 MILES | 9.7 KM | LEVEL 12 |

MAP: OS Explorer 108 Lower Tamar Valley & Plymouth

START/FINISH: Cremyll car park, grid ref: SX 453534. Alternatively reach Cremyll by ferry from the Plymouth side. Daily service between Admiral's Hard, Stonehouse, Plymouth and Cremyll

PATHS: good throughout, muddy in places in wet weather, 5 stiles

LANDSCAPE: wooded shoreline of tidal creek, fields, woods and coast

PUBLIC TOILETS: Cremyll

TOURIST INFORMATION: Plymouth, tel 01752 304849

THE PUB: Edgcumbe Arms, Cremyll

 Waterside paths – keep children supervised

Getting to the start

On the Cornish side Cremyll is best approached from the A38 between Saltash and Liskeard, taking the A374 towards Torpoint, then the B3247 following signs for Mount Edgcumbe Country Park. The car park is on the left as you enter Cremyll. For most it is simplest to take the ferry from Plymouth. From the city centre, follow signs for Torpoint and the Torpoint ferry, for 'Mount Edgcumbe via Cremyll ferry'. When facing the ferry slipway there is a left turn for the free car park.

Researched and written by: Des Hannigan, Brian Pearse

3 Go through the kissing gate opposite, signposted '**Maker Church, Kingsand**'. Follow the track ahead for 55yds (50m), then bear right, up the open field (no obvious path) heading between telegraph poles, to find a faint path leading to a kissing gate into into **Pigshill Wood**. Bear right along a track, go left at signposts and climb uphill following footpath signs. Cross a track, then go up some stone steps to reach more steps onto a public road. Cross, with care, and follow a path to **Maker Church**.

4 Turn sharp right in front of the church, follow the field edge, then go over a stile on the left. Follow the next field edge and cross a stile on the left, then follow the path past a **house** and across a lane into a field. Cross two fields to a lane. Turn left down the lane.

5 Pass **Hooe Lake Cottage** at the bottom and turn left to join the **coast path**, signposted just a few paces along the lane. Keep to the upper path at a junction, then merge with another track from the left and continue through the **woods**.

6 After a **folly shelter** the path zig-zags steeply up through the woods to the left to avoid a landslip. At the **ruined stone shelter** at the top turn right and drop back down through the woods. Cross the main track again and take a path zig-zagging steeply downhill to the coast. Follow the coast path signs back to **Mount Edgcumbe** and **Cremyll**.

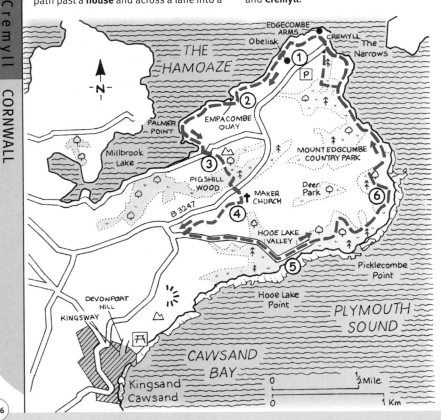

Edgcumbe Arms

The inn dates from the 15th century and is on the Tamar Estuary, next to Mount Edgcumbe Country Park, and close to the foot ferry from Plymouth. Views from the bow window seats and waterside terrace are glorious, taking in Drake's Island, the Royal William Yard and the marina. Real ales from St Austell and home-cooked food are served in a series of rooms, which are full of character with American oak panelling, deep leather sofas, log fires and stone flagged floors.

Food
Fresh local seafood and Cornish steaks are a feature of the menus alongside a daily curry and steak and ale pie. A good choice of bar snacks is also available.

Family facilities
Families will find a genuine welcome to children. There are two family bedrooms, a specified family area in the bar, high chairs and a children's menu.

Alternative refreshment stops
The Orangery Restaurant and Tea Room is in the Old Orangery in Mount Edgcumbe estate's Italian garden.

☞ Where to go from here
Catch the ferry across to Plymouth and follow the Waterfront Walkway to The Hoe and the Plymouth Dome, a high-tech visitor centre that lets you explore the sounds and smells of an Elizabethan Street, walk the gun-deck of a galleon, dodge the press gang, and witness the devastation of the Blitz (www.plymouthdome.Info). In Cornwall, head for Anthony House near Torpoint to view a fine, largely unaltered 18th-century mansion, which contains contemporary furniture and family portraits (www.nationaltrust.org.uk). Children will love the Monkey Sanctuary near Looe, where they can see a colony of Amazonian woolly monkeys in extensive indoor and outdoor territory (www.monkeysanctuary.org).

about the pub

Edgcumbe Arms
Cremyll, Torpoint
Cornwall PL10 1HX
Tel 01752 822294
www.smallandfriendlyinns.co.uk

DIRECTIONS:	see Getting to the start
PARKING:	use public car park
OPEN:	daily; all day (except early Jan to end Feb)
FOOD:	daily
BREWERY/COMPANY:	St Austell Brewery
REAL ALE:	St Austell Tribute, Tinner's Ale and HSD
DOGS:	allowed in the bars
ROOMS:	6 en suite

Around Brent Tor

A climb up to the Church of St Michael de Rupe at Brent Tor in West Devon.

Brent Tor

Anyone exploring western Dartmoor cannot fail to notice a conical peak, topped with a tower, protruding high above the rolling fields and woodlands towards the Cornish border. This strange natural formation is Brent Tor and, surprisingly, has nothing to do with the granite tors of Dartmoor. It is a remnant of the mass of lava that poured out onto the seabed here over 300 million years ago, when the area was a shallow sea. The softer rocks around have been eroded away over the millennia, leaving behind this extraordinary landmark 1,100ft (334m) above sea level. The name is thought to derive either from Ango-Saxon *brene* meaning 'beacon' or the Celtic *bryn* (hill or mound). Lying just inside the National Park boundary, it provides the perfect focus for a relaxing exploration of this quiet corner of West Devon.

The 13th-century Church of St Michael de Rupe ('of the rock') was originally built in

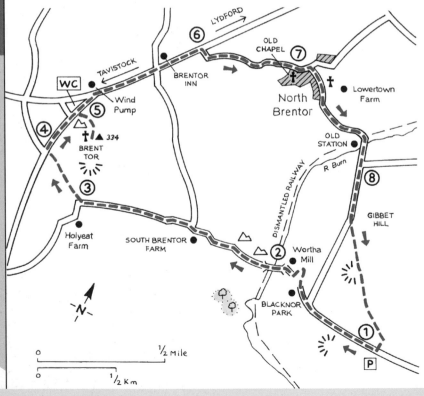

around 1130. Rebuilt towards the end of the 13th century, the tower was added during the 15th century. Services are held on Sunday evenings from Easter to September, and the views from here are breathtaking.

North Brentor was added to the parish in 1880, and all burials then took place at Christ Church in the village, since the soil on top of Brent Tor was too thin to accommodate a decent grave.

the walk

1 Walk straight ahead from your car towards **Brent Tor**, which positively invites you to visit it. Where the lane veers right turn left along an unfenced lane (dead end and weak bridge signs). Go gently downhill and over a **cattle grid**. The tarmac lane becomes a gravelly track and passes **Blacknor Park** (left), to cross the old railway line.

2 The stony track runs steeply uphill, levels off and runs into a green lane. At the next T-junction of tracks turn left to pass **South Brentor Farm** and a lane (right), and keep straight on slightly uphill – under beech trees – to pass 'Hillside' on the left.

3 Just past two **cottages** on the left the lane bends sharp left. Turn right through a metal gate following the bridleway marker along the bottom of the field, keeping the hedge left. Brent Tor is above to the right. Pass through **double metal gates** to meet the Tavistock to Lydford road – take care, there is fast traffic on this road.

The Church of St Michael, on the hill of Brent Tor

2h00 — **4 MILES** — **6.4 KM** — **LEVEL 123**

MAP:	OS Explorer 112 Launceston & Holsworthy
START/FINISH:	lay-by past cattle grid outside Mary Tavy on moorland road to North Brentor village, grid ref: SX 495800
PATHS:	tracks and green lanes, open fields and lanes
LANDSCAPE:	open moorland and rolling farmland
PUBLIC TOILETS.	at car park, Brent Tor
TOURIST INFORMATION:	Tavistock, tel 01822 612938
THE PUB:	Brentor Inn, North Brentor

🚷 One steep climb up Brent Tor

Getting to the start

The walk starts near Mary Tavy, which is about 5 miles north of Tavistock on the A386. Turn left at the garage in Mary Tavy, following the Brentor signs. In 0.5 mile (800m), cross a cattle grid onto open moorland. Park on the moorland to the right or in the small lay-by a little down the road on the left.

Researched and written by:
Brian Pearse, Sue Viccars

4 Turn right to reach the car park, toilets and **information board** for Brent Tor on the left.

5 Turn right and take the steep path up to the **church** – it's always windy up here – then retrace your steps to the road and turn right to pass **Brentor Inn** on your left.

6 When you reach **two white cottages** on either side of the road, turn right down a tarmac lane signposted '**Brentor and Mary Tavy**'. The lane runs gently downhill, with the moor rising steeply up behind the village ahead. This western edge of the moor is very different from the eastern side, where there is usually a long drive-in along wooded river valleys.

7 At the edge of the houses go straight on, keeping the old chapel right, until you reach the 1914–18 **war memorial**. Turn right slightly downhill to pass the phone box, church and village hall. Follow the lane

Looking south east from Brent Tor

what to look for

Just south west of Brent Tor is an enclosed area of mounds and depressions, all that remains of a 19th-century manganese mine, a major source of employment from 1815 to 1856. The manganese was used in the production of glass, bleach and steel, and was shipped out down the River Tamar from Morwellham Quay.

as it veers right to cross the **old railway line**. You can see the old station complete with platform canopy below you to the right.

8 Pass over the cattle grid onto the open moor, and up the lane. Where the lane bends right and you see two big **granite gateposts** in the beech-lined wall right, cut left diagonally over the edge of **Gibbet Hill** on an indistinct grassy track. The lane leads back to the car, but this is a more pleasant route. At the crest of the hill you will see your route back to your car on the lane below to the right.

Brentor Inn

about the pub

Brentor Inn
North Brentor, Tavistock
Devon PL19 0NF
Tel 01822 811001
www.brentorinn.com

DIRECTIONS: just after Point 5, before the turning to North Brentor	
PARKING: 60	
OPEN: all day; closed Monday	
FOOD: daily	
BREWERY/COMPANY: free house	
REAL ALE: St Austell Tinner's Ale, guest beers	
DOGS: allowed inside	

Set beside the lonely and windswept road between Lydford and Tavistock, this white-painted inn dates from the early 1800s and enjoys wonderful, far-reaching views across Dartmoor, up to Brent Tor (the focus of this walk), and into Cornwall from its beer garden. Spruced up following a period of neglect and then closure, the pub's single bar sports old flagstones, thick stone walls, dark wood pub furnishings and two warming winter fires.

Food
Hearty walking appetites will be satisfied by the range of traditional bar meals on offer, namely home-cooked pies, fresh fish and chips and lunchtime sandwiches.

Family facilities
Children are welcome in the conservatory dining area where they can order smaller portions of the main menu dishes

Alternative refreshment stops
If you drive north to Lydford go to the 16th-century Castle Inn (hotel and restaurant). There is also a National Trust restaurant at Lydford Gorge.

☞ Where to go from here
Visit Lydford, signposted off the A386 to the north. It was a Saxon fortress town, with its own mint in the 9th century. Lydford Castle, actually the moor's infamous stannery prison, is worth a visit. Just down the road is the National Trust's Lydford Gorge, where the crashing waterfalls and whirlpools of the River Lyd – the most impressive being the Devil's Cauldron – can be seen from a number of woodland walks. The 98ft (30m) White Lady waterfall is spectacular (www.nationaltrust.org.uk).

The Granite Way

A glorious, easy ride along an old railway line around the northwestern edge of Dartmoor, with an optional hilly extension to Bridestowe and historic Lydford.

Okehampton Castle and Lydford Gorge

The atmospheric ruins of Okehampton's Norman castle – once the largest in Devon – peep through the trees north of the line near the start of this ride. Built soon after the Norman Conquest, most of what can be seen today dates from the 13th and 15th centuries. The castle – seat of the Earls of Devon in medieval times – is beautifully situated on the banks of the West Okement River, with walks and picnic areas near by. It lies at one end of the Two Castles Trail, a 24-mile (39km) walking route linking it with the Norman castle at Launceston in east Cornwall.

At the other end of the ride lies Lydford, once an administrative centre for the Forest of Dartmoor. Lydford Castle, a tower built in the late 12th century as a prison and courtroom, was used by the Royalists in the Civil War. There's also the National Trust's Lydford Gorge. During the Ice Age the River Lyd carved a new and tortuous route through solid rock as it coursed west towards the River Tavy. The waters now hurtle through the 1.5 mile- (2.4km) long gorge via a succession of waterfalls and pools, including the beautiful 98ft (30m) White Lady waterfall. Various paths, some narrow and slippery, wend their way through the surrounding oak woodlands.

the ride

1 From Okehampton Station cross **Station Road** and keep ahead, as signed, parallel to the railway. After 50yds (46m) turn left onto a tarmac way that then bears right to run parallel to the railway. Follow this as it bears left under a bridge. Continue on to pass through a gate, left under the A30, through another gate, and right on the other side. The route bears away from the railway to reach **Meldon Quarry**, which started 200 years ago to produce a variety of materials, including 'Hornfells' used in construction work, and which was exposed when the railway cuttings were dug.

2 The next stop is **old Meldon Station** with its visitor centre. There's a buffet in a couple of old railway carriages, and a picnic area, with glorious views over Meldon's steel viaduct and towards Dartmoor's highest ground. The Devon and Cornwall Railway reached Okehampton in 1871 and was absorbed into the London and South Western Railway the following year. The line was extended to Lydford via the viaduct (which soars 150ft/46m over the West Okement Valley) in 1874, and

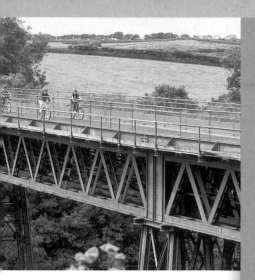

| 4h00 | 18 MILES | 29 KM | LEVEL 123 |

SHORTER ALTERNATIVE ROUTE

| 2h15 | 11 MILES | 17.7 KM | LEVEL 123 |

MAP: OS Explorer OL28 Dartmoor

START/FINISH: Okehampton Station, grid ref: SX 591944

TRAILS/TRACKS: level tarmac track, rough bridlepath to Bearslake Inn, narrow lanes/level track to Lydford

LANDSCAPE: moorland edge, farmland, woodland

PUBLIC TOILETS: at start and in Lydford

TOURIST INFORMATION: Okehampton, tel 01837 53020

CYCLE HIRE: YHA, Okehampton Station, tel 01837 53916

THE PUB: The Bearslake Inn, Lake

🅛 Crossing of A386 on Lydford extension, steep descent/ascent into/out of Bridestowe

Getting to the start

Okehampton lies off the A30 on the northern edge of Dartmoor. Make your way to the town centre and follow signs for the railway station

Why do this cycle ride?

There are so many options on this ride that it's hard to know which to recommend! It really is a route to suit all tastes and abilities. Quite apart from traversing stunningly beautiful landscapes, here are several possible picnic and refreshment stops along the way. Keen cyclists can extend the route via quiet country lanes to rejoin the old railway line and continue on to Lydford.

Researched and written by: Sue Viccars

closed to commercial passenger traffic in 1968. Today the 'Dartmoor Pony' runs out here from Okehampton on weekends and during the summer holidays.

3 Continue on over the **viaduct** – a fantastic ride, but take care in high winds (for Meldon Reservoir leave the route left just after the viaduct; on reaching the lane go straight over). Pass through a long cutting on the edge of **Prewley Moor**, after which views open up towards Sourton Tor (unusually formed of basalt, not granite). Cross the access lane to **Prewley Works**, and pass the pretty church of St Thomas à Becket at Sourton. The Highwayman pub can be accessed over the A386 here. Continue on through a short gated section at **Albrae**, and on past ponds to reach **Lake Viaduct**, built of local stone in 1874, and more lovely views.

4 Here you have a choice. The line ends 0.75 mile (1.2km) further on at **Southerly Halt picnic site**, so you can cycle on and turn round there. If you want to either go to **The Bearslake Inn**, or onto Lydford, turn left off the track just after the viaduct and descend steeply to a gate. Turn

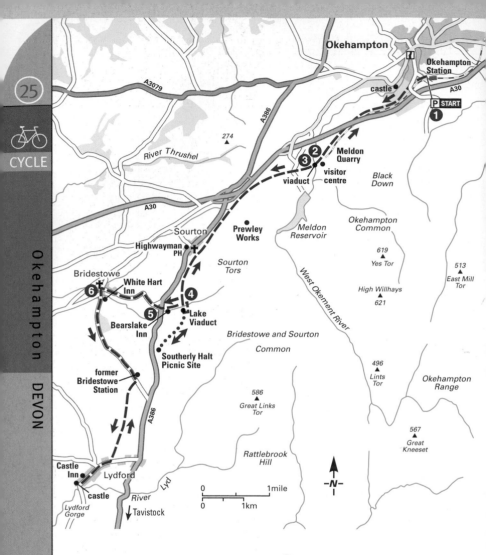

left under the **viaduct** and follow this rough track downhill to meet the A396. Turn left into the grounds of the pub, originally a 13th-century longhouse.

5 To continue to the ancient Saxon burgh of Lydford, cross the A386 – take great care – and cycle up the quiet lane opposite. At the T-junction turn left and follow the lane downhill into **Bridestowe**.

6 Turn left opposite the church, passing the White Hart Inn on the left. Cycle up Station Road (steep) and follow this for 1.5 miles (2.4km) to **old Bridestowe Station**. Cross the bridge and turn right onto the old railway track again. Follow this to Lydford. Leave the track and turn right down the road for the Castle Inn, castle and **Lydford Gorge**. Retrace your route back to Okehampton.

The Bearslake Inn

Standing on the edge of the National Park and built as a farm in the 13th century, this thatched and stone-built Devon longhouse is conveniently located beside the Granite Way cycle trail. Oozing old-world charm and character, expect to find flagstone floors, exposed beams and timbers, head-crackingly low ceilings, old pews, and a fine inglenook fireplace with crackling log fire in the rambling interior. Food is freshly prepared on the premises using local produce, including fish landed at Plymouth Quay and Taw Valley cheeses. Cyclists are very welcome and there's plenty of space in both the front and rear gardens to rest and relax on fine summer days.

Food
Lunchtime snacks take in sandwiches and filled baguettes (hot sausage and onion), traditional ploughman's with Taw Valley Brie, home-made soups, salads and the Bearslake burger with chips. Imaginative evening meals range from salmon and broccoli tart and beef casserole to chargrilled mackerel and whole baked sea bass.

Family facilities
Although children are not allowed in the bar there are two family dining areas. Smaller portions are available and children are welcome overnight.

Alternative refreshment stops
Plenty of pubs and cafés in Okehampton and the eccentric Highwayman Inn at Sourton. If continuing to Lydford, you'll pass the White Hart in Bridestow and the Castle Inn in Lydford.

about the pub

The Bearslake Inn
Lake, Sourton, Okehampton
Devon EX20 4HQ
Tel: 01837 861334
www.bearslakeinn.com

DIRECTIONS: pub is situated north of Lydford on the A386 Okehampton to Tavistock road

PARKING: 18

OPEN: daily; all day Sunday; all day all week June to September

FOOD: daily

BREWERY/COMPANY: free house

REAL ALE: Teignworthy Golden Sands and Reel Ale, Otter Nitter, Summerskills Best, guest beers

ROOMS: 5 en suite

☛ Where to go from here
Discover how people lived, worked and played on and around Dartmoor at the Museum of Dartmoor Life in Okehampton, housed on three floors in a 19th-century mill (www.museumofdartmoorlife.co.uk). Visit Okehampton Castle and enjoy the free audio tour which brings this romantic ruin to life (www.english-heritage.org.uk). Daily demonstrations at the Finch Foundry Working Museum in Sticklepath show how water-powered hammers made sickles, scythes and other hand tools. In Lydford, explore the spectacular gorge formed by the River Lyd (www.nationaltrust.org.uk), and look round Lydford Castle, a 12th-century tower that was once a notorious prison.

The Plym Valley trail

A pleasant ride along the line of the old Plym Valley railway, with an optional extension to the National Trust's magnificent house and parkland at Saltram.

Plym Bridge Woods and Blaxton Meadow

This railway line opened in 1859 under the South Devon and Tavistock Railway, and ran for 16 miles (25.7km) from Plymouth to Tavistock. The cycle route through Plym Bridge Woods is one of the best bits. The woods became popular with daytrippers who alighted at Plym Bridge Halt, built in 1906 (on the site of the car park mentioned in Point 5). You'll also see evidence of industrial activity: there were several quarries here, workers' cottages, a small lead/silver mine, a canal and three railway lines. The remains of 18th-century Rumple Quarry – from which slate was extracted – and engine house are passed on the right, soon after entering the woods. Plym Bridge Woods are particularly lovely in spring, thick with wood anenomes, primroses, bluebells and ransoms.

Once in the Saltram estate you soon pass Blaxton Meadow on your right, an area of managed saltmarsh on the Plym Estuary. It was enclosed in 1886 and developed as agricultural land, and around the time of World War Two supported a cricket ground! Plans to regenerate the saltmarsh started in 1995, and today it provides suitable habitats for a wide range of flora and fauna, with large numbers of migrant waders; look out for flocks of curlews in winter, and deep red samphire beds in autumn.

the ride

1 Return to the lane, turn right and descend into Clearbrook and continue past **The Skylark Inn** for about 500yds (457m). Turn right opposite the village hall on a track. After 100yds (91m) turn right up a steep, narrow path; at the top by the **pylon** bear left downhill (cyclists should dismount). This turns sharp left, then right through a gate onto the rough, gritty, old railway line. Follow this for about 0.5 mile (0.8km) to **Goodameavy**, where tarmac takes over. (Note: to avoid this initial rough section turn left at the fork by the parking area, signed 'Goodameavy', and cycle steeply downhill to join the railway.)

2 Soon after Goodameavy the track passes through **Shaugh Tunnel** (note: there are lights, but these are turned off between dusk and dawn – there's a colony of roosting bats in the tunnel), and then under an aqueduct. Pass Shaugh Bridge Halt and cross **Ham Green viaduct**; look back left and you'll catch sight of the Dewerstone Rock above the wooded Plym Valley just above its junction with the River Meavy.

3 At **Ham Bridge** the route meets a lane; turn right uphill towards **Bickleigh**. At the T-junction turn left and proceed very steeply downhill (young children should dismount). Turn right on a narrow wooded path back onto the railway line and continue through deciduous woodland. Pass over Bickleigh viaduct and into the National Trust's **Plym Bridge Woods**. Continue over Cann viaduct – look over the left side to see the remains of Rumple wheelpit by the river below, and the face of **Cann Quarry** beyond.

4 At Plym Bridge follow signs sharp left to leave the track. For a picnic by the river, turn left under the railway towards the 18th-century bridge; the meadow is on the right (leave your bikes on the lane). For **Saltram House** – created in the 18th century with 500 acres (202ha) of parkland – cross the car park entrance and turn right on a level woodland track. Cycle towards Plymouth (note that Plymouth is one end of the Devon Coast to Coast route, which runs for 102 miles/163km to Ilfracombe – watch out for serious and speedy cyclists!) to emerge by **Coypool Park-and-Ride** on the right.

5 Cross the road at the T-junction and follow the narrow path ahead (barrier); cross the next road and take the rough track opposite. Just past the **playing field gates** (right) bear right on a narrow path to emerge under the A38. Bear diagonally right to find a railed tarmac path uphill left. Follow that up and down, then along the edge of the Plym Estuary to reach the National Trust's **Saltram Estate**.

6 At the edge of parkland keep right, and follow the estuary to **Point Cottage**. Turn left inland on an estate lane to cross the parking area, with the house and **shop** left. At the signpost bear left, signed **'Riverside walk and bird hide'** and cycle carefully downhill, avoiding pedestrians, keeping straight on where the tarmac way bears left towards offices. Re-enter the **parkland** and keep ahead to rejoin the outward route.

| 3h00 | 13.5 MILES | 21.7 KM | LEVEL 1**2**3 |

SHORTER ALTERNATIVE ROUTE

| 2h15 | 10.5 MILES | 16.9 KM | LEVEL 1**2**3 |

MAP: OS Explorer OL20 South Devon

START/FINISH: Clearbook parking area above village, grid ref SX 518650

TRAILS/TRACKS: mix of bumpy and well-surfaced track

LANDSCAPE: wooded valley, townscape, estuary and parkland on extension

PUBLIC TOILETS: Coypool (Point 5)

TOURIST INFORMATION: Plymouth, tel 01752 304849

CYCLE HIRE: Tavistock Cycles, Tavistock, tel 01822 617630

THE PUB: The Skylark Inn, Clearbrook

🛈 First 0.75 mile (1.2km) rough and bumpy (alternative lane access given), steep hills at Bickleigh and busy roads on extension

Getting to the start

Clearbrook lies on Dartmoor's western edge, clearly signposted off the A386 Tavistock to Plymouth road, 2.5 miles (4km) south of Yelverton. Follow the lane across the down and park at the furthest parking area on the right where the road forks.

Why do this cycle ride?

This ride – particularly if the extension to Saltram House is included – covers an impressive range of landscapes: moorland, woodland, river estuary and parkland. The views at both the northern (Dartmoor) and southern (Plym Estuary) ends are impressive, and the outskirts of Plymouth, for Saltram House, passed quickly.

Researched and written by: Sue Viccars

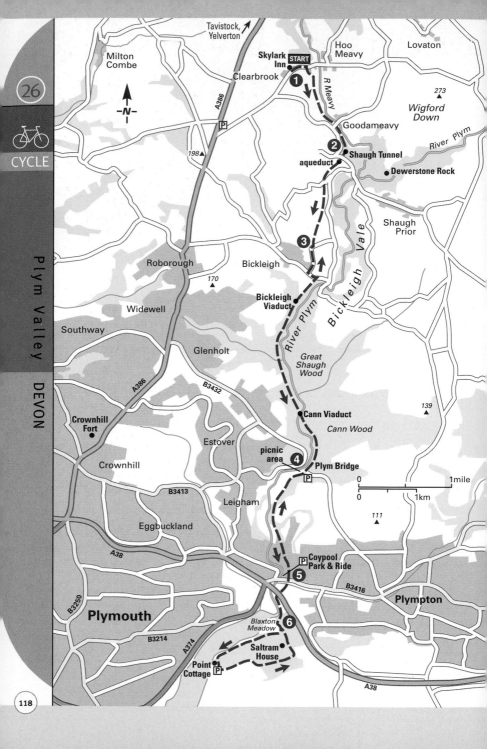

Plym Valley DEVON

Tavistock, Yelverton

Milton Combe

Hoo Meavy

Lovaton

Skylark Inn START
1

Clearbrook

R Meavy

Goodameavy

273

Wigford Down

River Plym

2 Shaugh Tunnel

aqueduct

Dewerstone Rock

A386

198

Shaugh Prior

3

Shaugh Vale

Roborough

Bickleigh

170

Bickleigh Viaduct

Widewell

River Plym

Southway

Bickleigh Vale

Glenholt

Great Shaugh Wood

B3432

139

Cann Viaduct

Cann Wood

Crownhill Fort

A386

Estover

picnic area

4 Plym Bridge

Crownhill

0   1mile

B3413

0   1km

Leigham

111

Eggbuckland

A38

Coypool Park & Ride

5

B3416

Plympton

B3250

Plymouth

B3214

A374

Blaxton Meadow

6

Saltram House

Point Cottage

A38

The Skylark Inn

Although only minutes from Plymouth, you will find the Skylark tucked away in a pretty row of cottages in a sleepy village on the southern flanks of Dartmoor. It's a welcoming two-room pub, the beamed main bar is simply furnished and boasts a big fireplace with wood-burning stove. Although very much a lively local the pub also bustles with passing walkers and cyclists exploring the National Park. Large back garden for summer alfresco eating and drinking.

Food

Good wholesome food is served from an extensive menu that features hot pasties, beef sandwiches, battered cod with chips, pasta meals, short-crust pastry pies, lamb tagine and vegetable stew with dumplings. Sunday roast lunches.

Family facilities

Children are welcome in the rear family room (no under 14s in the bar). There's a children's menu and an adventure play area in the garden.

Alternative refreshment stops

There is a licensed café at Saltram House.

☞ Where to go from here

At Buckland Monachorum you'll find Buckland Abbey, formerly a 13th-century Cistercian Abbey, which was sold to Sir Francis Drake in 1581. He lived here until his death in 1596. Restored buildings house a fascinating exhibition about the abbey's history, including Drake's drum (www.nationaltrust.org.uk). At the National Marine Aquarium in Plymouth, Britain's biggest aquarium, you can see 15 species of shark and ray, walk through an underwater tunnel and enter the Twilight Zone (www.national-aquarium.co.uk). Discover Plymouth's past and much more at the Plymouth Dome, a high-tech visitor centre with audio-visual commentaries and observation galleries (www.plymouthdome.gov.uk). If you visit Saltram House by bike, your entry fee is refunded (www.nationaltrust.org.uk).

about the pub

The Skylark Inn

Clearbrook, Yelverton
Devon PL20 6JD
Tel 01822 853258
www.theskylarkinn.co.uk

DIRECTIONS: see Getting to the start; descend into Clearbrook and the Skylark Inn is on the left

PARKING: 16

OPEN: daily; all day Saturday and Sunday

FOOD: daily; all day Saturday and Sunday

BREWERY/COMPANY: Unique Inns

REAL ALE: Courage Best, Sharp's Special, Bass, Clearbrook Ale

The Princetown railway

Princetown

A tough ride through the wilds of Dartmoor, along the old route of the Princetown to Yelverton railway.

Quarrying round Princetown

There's a long history of quarrying granite on Dartmoor. Quarrying began around 1820 at both Haytor Quarry, under George Templer, and (in direct competition) at Swelltor and Foggintor, under Thomas Trywhitt (who also built roads and many buildings in the Princetown area, including the Plume of Feathers Inn in 1785). Foggintor (originally known as Royal Oak) ceased working around 1900, and Swelltor

in 1921. Both reopened for a while in 1937, in response to an increase in demand for roadstone. Foggintor supplied granite for Dartmoor Prison, and local granite was also used in Nelson's Column in Trafalgar Square, London. Look towards Foggintor (Point 3) and you'll see various ruined buildings: as well as cottages, there was also a chapel used as a school. The old quarry workings are now flooded and provide a peaceful picnic spot.

Merrivale Quarry (originally Tor Quarry), a little further along the route, was the last working quarry on Dartmoor, operating from 1875 to 1997. Granite blocks from the old London Bridge were re-dressed here when the bridge was sold to the USA, and

1h45 **5 MILES** **8 KM** **LEVEL 1 2 3**

stone was also used in the war memorial in the Falklands after the war in 1982.

the ride

1 Turn left out of the car park along the rough road. Just past the **fire station** (left) bear left as signed (disused railway/Tyrwhitt Trail) on a narrow fenced path, which bears right. Go through a gate. The path widens to a gritty track, and passes a **coniferous plantation** (right).

2 Suddenly you're out in the open on a long embankment, looking towards the forests around **Burrator Reservoir** ahead right, below **Sheeps Tor** (left) and **Sharpitor** (right). Continue along the contours of the hill – it's quite rough – as you progress look ahead left to the railway winding its way towards **Ingra Tor**. This is the old Plymouth and Dartmoor railway line, brainchild of Sir Thomas Tyrwhitt, friend of and private secretary to the Prince Regent. Originally a tramway with horse-drawn wagons, it opened in 1823. It was part of Tyrwhitt's plans to exploit the area's natural resources (granite), at the same time enabling materials such as coal and lime to be brought to Princetown more easily. The Princetown Railway Company (a subsidiary of the GWR) took it over in 1881; it reopened as a steam railway in 1883, but was never profitable and closed in 1956. However, it's a great footpath and cycle track.

MAP: OS Explorer OL28 Dartmoor

START/FINISH: Princetown car park (contributions), grid ref: SX 588735

TRAILS/TRACKS: rocky former railway track and one particularly steep and rough section

LANDSCAPE: open moorland

PUBLIC TOILETS: at start

TOURIST INFORMATION: High Moorland Visitor Centre, Princetown, tel 01822 890414

CYCLE HIRE: Runnage Farm, Postbridge (plus camping barn), tel 01822 880222

THE PUB: Dartmoor Inn, near Princetown

🛑 Only suitable for older children with mountain bikes

Getting to the start

Princetown lies on the B3212 between Two Bridges and Yelverton, on Dartmoor. From Two Bridges, turn right in the middle of the town; from Yelverton, turn left (High Moorland Visitor Centre on the corner), following signs for the car park.

Why do this cycle ride?

This is a rather different sort of ride, and one that will test both your bike and your concentration! It follows the line of the old Princetown to Yelverton railway, but has not been surfaced. It's suitable for families with older children and those who have mountain bikes, and you'll have to push your bikes up one particularly rough section. But for a taste of Dartmoor 'proper', it's hard to beat.

Researched and written by: Sue Viccars

Top: The Dartmoor Inn at Merrivale Bridge
Left: Walkers on the trail

3 Reach the edge of **Foggintor Quarry** (left), with Swelltor Quarry on the hill ahead; a track crosses the trail. The site of King Tor Halt (1928), from where a siding led to Foggintor, is near by. Keep straight ahead, almost immediately taking the left fork (the track becomes grassier). Look right towards the spoil heaps of Foggintor Quarry. Follow the track on – look left towards Merrivale Quarry (the Dartmoor Inn is just out of sight below) – try to spot the Bronze Age **Merrivale stone rows**. Follow the track as it bears left round the hill (below King's Tor Quarry), to enjoy views right over **Vixen Tor**, almost 100ft (30m) high, home to one of the moor's most evil characters, the witch Vixana. Pass through a cutting – another branch joins right – and keep on to another fork.

4 Keep right along the lower track; views change again, with the wooded **Walkham Valley** below right and – on a

good day – the sparkling waters of Plymouth Sound in the distance. About 50yds (46m) beyond the fork look left to see a pile of dressed stone on the upper track: 12 granite corbels, cut in 1903 for work on London Bridge, but excess to requirements. Pass the spoil heaps of **Swelltor Quarry**; the track is now fenced on the right, with views ahead to the bridge en route for **Ingra Tor**.

5 Where the track starts to curve sharp right, turn left opposite an old gate. Push your bike up a rough, rocky track to regain the outward route near **Foggintor Quarry**.

6 Turn right and make your way bumpily back to **Princetown**. The building of the infamous prison in 1806 – originally for French prisoners from the Napoleonic wars – was also down to Trywhitt. Since 1850 it has been a civilian establishment.

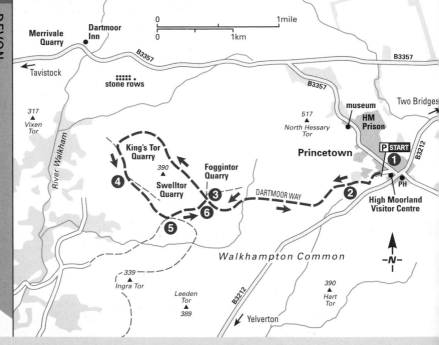

Dartmoor Inn

Situated at 1,000ft (305m) above sea level, this whitewashed old inn enjoys sweeping views across moorland and the Walkham Valley, and on a clear evening the lights of Plymouth and the Eddystone Lighthouse can be seen. Originally quarryman's cottages built in the 17th century, the pub was once part of the Walreddon Manor Estate and has been a pub since at least 1852. A roaring log fire in a big stone fireplace is a welcome sight in the largely open-plan and partly carpeted main bar. On fine summer days soak up the view with a pint at one of the picnic benches on the grassy area to the front of the pub.

Food

Traditional bar meals range from salads, ploughman's and filled baps, to chicken, ham and mushroom pie, gammon steak and jam sponge and custard. Evening dishes take in grills, pasta meals and specialities like rack of lamb and steak au poivre.

Family facilities

Although there are no special facilities for children, families are made very welcome at the pub.

Alternative refreshment stops

Pubs and tea rooms in Princetown.

about the pub

Dartmoor Inn
Merrivale Bridge, Princetown
Devon PL20 6ST
Tel: 01822 890340

DIRECTIONS: load up bikes, turn left out of the car park, pass the prison and turn left again at the T-junction with the B3357, the pub is on the right in 1.5 miles (3km)
PARKING: 25
OPEN: closed Sunday evening, Monday and Tuesday between November and Easter
FOOD: daily
BREWERY/COMPANY: free house
REAL ALE: Marston's Pedigree, Bass, guest beer
ROOMS: 3 bedrooms, 2 en suite

☞ Where to go from here

To discover more about the history of Dartmoor, and what to see and do in the area, visit the High Moorland Visitor Centre in Princetown (www.dartmoor-npa.gov.uk). Young children will enjoy a visit to Dartmoor's Miniature Pony and Animal Farm near Moretonhampstead, where they can see ponies, donkeys, pigs and lambs at close quarters, and there are nature trails and indoor and outdoor play areas (www.miniatureponycentre.com). Discover the rugged beauty of the Bovey Valley at the Becky Falls Woodland Park (www.beckyfalls-dartmoor.com), and the world of otters and butterflies at the fascinating Buckfast Butterfly Farm and Dartmoor Otter Sanctuary (www.ottersandbutterflies.co.uk).

Bigbury-on-Sea and Burgh Island

WALK

A chance to mingle with the stars in an art deco dream and have a drink in Devon's oldest inn.

Bigbury and Burgh Island

The broad, sandy beaches and dunes at Bigbury-on-Sea and Bantham, at the mouth of the River Avon south of Kingsbridge, attract hundreds of holidaymakers every summer, drawn by the appeal of sun, sand and sea. There's no doubt that this is a perfect spot for a family day out. Gone are the days of the 16th or 17th centuries when Bigbury was merely famous for its catches of pilchards! But there's something else appealing about this part of the South Devon coast. Just off Bigbury beach, 307yds (282m) from shore, lies craggy Burgh Island, with its famous hotel gazing at the mainland. This extraordinary island is completely surrounded by the sea at high tide but is accessible via the weird and wonderful sea tractor that ploughs its way through the waters.

The island was known as la Burgh in the 15th century, and later Borough Island. There was a chapel dedicated to St Michael on its summit in 1411, and it has been likened to the much larger St Michael's Mount in Cornwall. The remains of a 'huer's hut' at the top of the island – a fisherman's lookout – is evidence of the times when pilchard fishing was a mainstay of life here too, hence the building of the Pilchard Inn, housed in one of the original fisherman's cottages. But it is the island's more recent history that is so fascinating. It was bought in 1929 by wealthy industrialist Archibald Nettlefold, who built the Burgh Island Hotel, much as we see it today. He ran it as

a guest house for friends and celebrities, and it became a highly fashionable venue for the jet-set in the 1930s. Noel Coward was among the famous who visited, and it is thought that Edward, Prince of Wales and Wallis Simpson escaped from the limelight here; but the island's most famous connection has to be with Agatha Christie.

Two of her books, *Evil Under the Sun* and *And Then There Were None*, were written here, and the influence of the hotel and its location on her writing is clear. By the mid 1980s the hotel had fallen into disrepair, and two London fashion consultants, Beatrice and Tony Porter, bought the island and restored the hotel to its original 1930s Art Deco glory, complete with the famous Palm Court and authentic Twenties cocktail bar. For a bit of escapism Burgh Island is hard to beat – but take your cheque book!

the walk

1 Leave the car park through the entrance. Follow **coast path signs** right (for the low tide route to the seasonal ferry to Bantham), then left towards the road,

1h45	3 MILES	4.8 KM	LEVEL 2

MAP: OS Explorer OL20 South Devon

START/FINISH: huge car park at Bigbury-on-Sea, grid ref: SX 651442

PATHS: fields, tracks (muddy in winter), coast path, 2 stiles

LANDSCAPE: rolling coastal farmland and cliff top

PUBLIC TOILETS: at car park

TOURIST INFORMATION: Kingsbridge, tel 01548 853195

THE PUB: Pilchard Inn, Burgh Island

🛈 Steep sections of narrow coast path close to the cliff edge

Getting to the start

Bigbury-on-Sea is signposted off the A379 between Plymouth and Kingsbridge. A mile (1.6km) east of Modbury, turn right on the B3392 towards Bigbury and Bigbury-on-Sea. On entering Bigbury-on-Sea there is a large pay-and-display car park by the beach on the left.

Researched and written by:
Brian Pearse, Sue Viccars

Above: Burgh Island is connected to the mainland by sands

then left again up a grassy area. Turn left before the **bungalow**, then left (unmarked path) to reach the road. Turn right and walk steeply uphill to **Mount Folly Farm**.

2 Turn left along a gravelly track (signed **'Ringmore'**). At the top of the field is a junction of paths; go through the gate, then through the metal gate ahead, keeping downhill by the hedge on your right. Walk downhill through a kissing gate. Cross the **farm track** and up the field, to reach a high stile, then descend steps into a narrow lane.

3 Cross over, following signs for **Ringmore**, through the left of the two gates. Walk down into the next combe, keeping the hedgebank right. Cross the stream at the bottom on a **concrete walkway**, and over a stile. Ignore the path left, but go straight ahead, uphill, through a **plantation** and gate onto a narrow path between a fence and hedge.

4 Pass through a kissing gate, then turn right. Turn immediately left uphill though a **metal gate/kissing gate** to join a track that leads to Ringmore. Turn right at

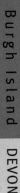
the lane, then left at the **church** to find the **Journey's End pub** on the right.

5 From the pub turn right down the narrow lane which gives way to a footpath. It winds round to meet a tarmac lane. Turn left downhill. Walk straight on down the track (signed to **'Lower Manor Farm'**) and keep going down past the **'National Trust Ayrmer Cove'** notice. After a small gate the track splits; keep left (unsigned) and straight on.

6 Turn left through a kissing gate and walk towards the cove on a grassy path above the combe (left). Pass through a gate

and over two stiles to gain the **beach**.

7 Follow coast path signs (**'Challaborough'**) left over a small footbridge then climb very steeply uphill to the cliff top and great views over Burgh Island. The cliffs are crumbly here – take care. The path is narrow, with a wire fence left, and leads to **Challaborough** – basically one huge holiday camp.

8 Turn right along the beach road and follow the track that leads uphill along the coast towards **Bigbury**. Go straight on to meet the tarmac road, then right on a narrow gravel path to the **car park**.

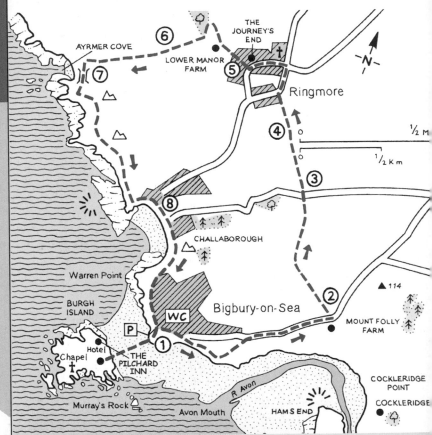

Pilchard Inn

Atmospheric 14th-century white-walled pub located on a tiny tidal island reached only by giant sea tractor when the tide is in – stroll across the sand when to tide is out. Once frequented by pirates and smugglers, the island is still said to be haunted by the notorious Tom Crocker who was shot outside the pub. Two rustic bars with a seafaring atmosphere, ancient exposed timbers, stone walls, blazing log fires and slate floors are furnished with old wooden settles. The main catch off the island was pilchard – hence the name.

Food

Unsurprisingly, seafood figures on the simple menu, which takes in fish soup, crab sandwiches, seafood risotto, and other sandwiches filled with beef and horseradish or chicken and avocado.

Family facilities

Children are welcome in the non-smoking bar and kid-sized sandwiches are available. When the tide is out, children can play on the sandy beach while mum and dad enjoy a drink on the beach-edge terrace.

Alternative refreshment stops

The wonderful Bay Café at Bigbury has great views over Burgh Island. There's Venus Café and a beach café at Challaborough. The Journey's End at Ringmore is full of atmosphere and has great food.

☛ Where to go from here

In the Old Grammar School in Kingsbridge is the Cookworthy Museum of Rural Life. Reconstructed room-sets of a Victorian kitchen, an Edwardian pharmacy, a

about the pub

Pilchard Inn
Burgh Island, Bigbury-on-Sea
Devon TQ7 4BG
Tel: 01548 810514
www.burghisland.com

DIRECTIONS: see Getting to the start (use tractor at high tide)

PARKING: start point car park

OPEN: daily; all day

FOOD: lunchtimes only (except summer evening barbeques Thursday to Saturday)

BREWERY/COMPANY: free house

REAL ALE: Teignworthy beers, Greene King Old Speckled Hen, Pilchard Bitter, guest beers

DOGS: allowed inside

costume room and an extensive collection of local historical Items are gathered here to illustrate South Devon life. Explore Totnes and its castle, one of the best surviving examples of a Norman motte and bailey castle with spectacular views, and take a steam train ride through the Dart Valley on the South Devon Railway (www.southdevonrailway.org).

Around Dartington Hall Estate

A gentle walk around the Dartington Hall Estate, with a pretty pub loop along the steam railway.

Dartington Estate

You could be forgiven for thinking that Dartington is really nothing more than what you see as you cross the roundabout on the A384 leading south from the A38 to Totnes – just somewhere you pass en route to the South Hams. But there's so much more to Dartington than that, and the story behind 'the vision' of Leonard and Dorothy Elmhirst, who bought the estate in 1925, is a fascinating one. This walk circles the estate and you should allow time at the end to visit its central buildings.

Dartington Hall was described by Nikolaus Pevsner in his classic book on the buildings of Devon as 'the most spectacular medieval mansion' in Devon. The great hall and main courtyard were built for John Holand, Duke of Exeter, at the end of the 14th century, and although all the buildings have since been carefully restored, to walk through the gateway into the courtyard today, with the superb Great Hall with its hammerbeam roof opposite, is to step back in time. Arthur Champernowne came to own the manor in 1554, and made various alterations, and the estate stayed in the hands of the Champernowne family until 1925. Further restoration work was carried out in Georgian times, but by the time the Elmhirsts came on the scene the Hall was derelict. Modern visitors can explore the Great Hall, courtyard and gardens, providing they are not in use, in return for a moderate fee.

St Mary's Church can be found on the northern edge of the estate just off the Totnes road. You'll pass the site of the original estate church just to the north of the Hall. It was demolished in 1873, leaving only the tower, which can be seen today. The new church, which is wonderfully light and spacious, was built in 1880, following the exact dimensions of the original building, and re-using various items from it, such as the south porch with its lovely star vault, the chancel screen, font, pulpit and roof. A tablet in the outer east wall records the rebuilding and subsequent consecration of the church by Frederick, Bishop of Exeter. The Dartington Hall Trust, a registered charity, was set up in 1935, and evolved from the vision of Leonard Elmhirst and his American wife Dorothy Whitney Straight, who bought the derelict hall and 1,000 acres (405ha) of the estate and set about making their dream reality. He was interested in farming and forestry, and in increasing employment opportunities in rural areas. She believed passionately in the arts as a way of promoting personal and social improvement. Their joint aim was to provide a foundation where both dreams could be realised simultaneously, and Dartington Hall today, home to Dartington College of Arts and a whole range of other educational facilities, provides the perfect setting.

the walk

1 From the car park turn left downhill. Follow the pavement until you reach the **River Dart**.

2 Turn left through a kissing gate (no footpath sign) and follow the river northwards. This part of the walk is likely to be very muddy after rainfall. The Dart here is broad, tree-lined and slow-moving. Pass through a **kissing gate,** through a strip of woodland and over another stile into the next meadow. At the end of that pass through another kissing gate onto a short **wooded track**.

3 Walk along the river edge of the next field (with **Park Copse** to your left). At the end of that field go through a kissing gate into **Staverton Ford Plantation**. Where the track veers sharply left go through the gate in the wall ahead, then right to follow a narrow, wooded path back towards the

Top: Steam train at Staverton station
Below: The stone Staverton Bridge

2h30	**5 MILES**	**8 KM**	**LEVEL 1**23

MAP: OS Explorer 110 Torquay & Dawlish
START/FINISH: opposite entrance to Dartington Hall, grid ref: SX 799628
PATHS: fields, woodland tracks and country lanes
LANDSCAPE: river meadows, parkland and mixed woodland
PUBLIC TOILETS: outside entrance to Dartington Hall and Staverton village
TOURIST INFORMATION: Totnes, tel 01803 863168
THE PUB: The Sea Trout Inn, Staverton
🚫 Dogs not allowed within Dartington Hall grounds

Getting to the start

Dartington is about 2 miles (3.2km) north west of Totnes on the A384. Follow signs for Dartington Hall. There are car parks on the left opposite the main entrance.

Researched and written by:
Brian Pearse, Sue Viccars

WALK

Dartington DEVON

Dartington

DEVON

river. Keep on this path as it runs parallel with the Dart, becoming a broad woodland track through **North Wood**. When you see buildings through the trees on the right, leave the track and walk downhill to a metal gate and a lane.

4 Turn right to cross **Staverton Bridge**. Before the level crossing turn right to pass through **Staverton Station yard** into a park-like area between the railway and river. Follow the path across the single-track railway and walk on to meet a lane by **Sweet William Cottage**.

5 Turn right and follow the lane to its end. Go straight ahead on a small gritty path to pass the **Church of St Paul de Leon**, who was a 9th-century travelling preacher. Turn left at the lane to pass the public toilets,

and left at the junction to **The Sea Trout Inn**. After your break retrace your steps to the metal gate past **Staverton Bridge**.

6 Turn immediately right to rejoin the track. Follow this until it runs downhill and bends left. Walk towards the gate on the right, then turn left on the narrow concrete path. The houses of **Huxham's Cross** can be seen right. Keep on the concrete path, which leaves the woodland to run between wire fences to meet a concrete drive at the **Dartington Crafts Education Centre**. Follow the drive to meet the road.

7 Turn left to pass **Old Parsonage Farm**. Keep on the road and pavements back to **Dartington Hall**, passing the gardens and ruins of the original church (right), until you see the **car park** on the left.

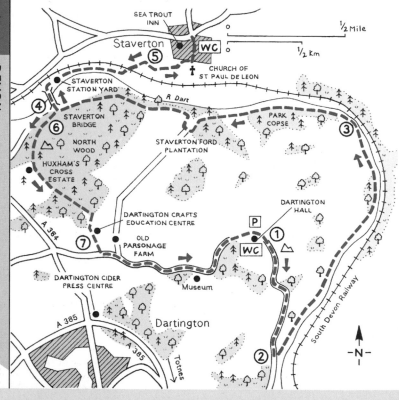

The Sea Trout Inn

Situated in the tranquil rural surroundings of the Dart Valley, this attractive 15th-century inn has a loyal local following. It's a rambling, whitewashed building with a relaxed atmosphere and a good combination of comfortable hotel, elegant restaurant and village pub serving cracking Palmer's beers. A fishing theme runs through the pub, some specimens mounted in showcases, others depicted in paintings or on plates. From the open-plan and plushly furnished main bar there's access to a sheltered, patio-style garden complete with pond and fountain. Separate public bar with pool table. Eleven comfortably furnished en suite bedrooms makes this an ideal base for touring Dartmoor and the South Devon coast.

Food
An interesting bar menu features sausage, kidney and bacon casserole with parsnip purée or rump steak with lyonnaise potatoes and béarnaise sauce, plus classics such as bangers and mash and gammon and egg.

Family facilities
Children are welcome in the eating area of the bar and restaurant and overnight in two family bedrooms. There's a children's menu and smaller portions are available.

Alternative refreshment stops
There are two excellent eateries at Dartington Cider Press Centre – Cranks vegetarian restaurant and Muffins, which provides light lunches in the open air. Within the grounds of Dartington Hall there is the White Hart restaurant and bar, where you can enjoy a drink in atmospheric surroundings.

about the pub

The Sea Trout Inn
Staverton, Totnes
Devon TQ9 6PA
Tel 01803 762274
www.seatroutinn.com

DIRECTIONS:	village signposted off the A384 between Dartington and the A38 at Buckfastleigh, see Point 5 of walk
PARKING:	80
OPEN:	daily
FOOD:	daily
BREWERY/COMPANY:	Palmer's Brewery
REAL ALE:	Palmer's IPA, Gold and Copper Ale
DOGS:	allowed inside
ROOMS:	11 en suite

☛ Where to go from here
Spend some time at the Cider Press Centre. There's farm food, a bookshop, woodturning, great refreshments, a cookshop, Dartington pottery shop, toy shop and plant centre. You can't fail to notice the steam trains running along the opposite side of the river. This is the South Devon Railway, which runs from Buckfastleigh to Totnes. The station at Buckfastleigh has old locomotives and rolling stock on display, a museum and café, riverside walks and a picnic area (www.southdevonrailway.org). Nearby is Buckfast Butterflies and Otter Sanctuary (www.ottersandbutterflies.co.uk), and Buckfast Abbey, a Benedictine monastery by the River Dart (www.buckfast.org).

East Portlemouth to Limebury Point

Only a short ferry trip apart, the contrasts across the Kingsbridge Estuary could not be greater.

Salcombe

Salcombe is a delightful place but very busy. To avoid the crowds you can follow this walk from the tiny hamlet of East Portlemouth, opposite the town, from where you get some of the best views in the area. Once the haunt of smugglers and pirates, Salcombe has a civilised, prosperous, and, as a result of its sheltered position and deep blue waters, an almost Mediterranean feel. It's smaller and gentler than Dartmouth, and popular with the sailing fraternity. The estuary is a marvellous place for young families, too.

At low tide there is a run of sandy beaches all along the East Portlemouth side, enabling those staying in Salcombe simply to hop on the ferry for a day on the beach. (Note: Many of these sandy coves are cut off at high tide – take care.)

From Limebury Point you can see across the estuary to Overbecks (National Trust), an elegant Edwardian house in a magnificent setting above South Sands

East Portlemouth has a totally different feel from Salcombe. It is small, quiet and unspoilt. During the 19th century half the population was evicted by the absentee landlord as a result of their preference for fishing and wrecking over working the land.

the walk

1 Park on the verge near the phone box at East Portlemouth (or in the parking area – contributions to village hall fund). Walk through the parking area and steeply downhill on a narrow tarmac footpath signposted 'Salcombe', which gives way to **steep steps**.

Below: Salcombe and its harbour
Below right: The sandy beach at Mill Bay

2h00 · **4** MILES · **6.4** KM · **LEVEL** 1 2 3

MAP: OS Explorer OL20 South Devon

START/FINISH: near phone box in East Portlemouth or in small parking bay, grid ref: SX 746385

PATHS: good coast path, field paths and tracks, no stiles

LANDSCAPE: river estuary, rocky coast and coves, farmland

PUBLIC TOILETS: at Mill Bay, passed on Points 3 and 7

TOURIST INFORMATION: Salcombe, tel 01548 843927

THE PUB: Victoria Inn, Salcombe

🔴 Undulating, sometimes steep and rocky, coastal path

Getting to the start

East Portlemouth is about 9 miles south east of Kingsbridge on very narrow and winding roads. From Kingsbridge take the A379 towards Dartmouth. In 4 miles (6.4km), turn right at Frogmore following signs for East Portlemouth for 5 miles (8km). Park on the roadside next to the telephone box, opposite a row of cottages. Alternatively park in the village car park straight ahead, with wonderful views over the Kingsbridge Estuary.

Researched and written by:
Brian Pearse, Sue Viccars

2 When you reach the lane at the bottom of the steps, turn right if you want to visit the Venus Café and catch the ferry to Salcombe. If you want to get on with the walk, turn left along the lane as it follows the edge of the estuary. This is the official route of the **coast path** and it passes some very exclusive residences in almost subtropical surroundings.

3 The lane leads to the pretty, sandy beach at **Mill Bay**. Follow the coast path signs for **Gara Rock** along the edge of a sycamore wood, with lovely views across the estuary, and glimpses of inviting little coves.

4 At **Limebury Point** you reach open cliff, with great views to South Sands and Overbecks opposite and craggy Bolt Head. The coast path now veers eastwards below **Portlemouth Down**, which was divided into strip fields in the late 19th century.

5 The path along this stretch undulates steeply, and is rocky in places. Keep going until you reach the bench and viewpoint over the beach at **Rickham Sands**. Just beyond this, as the coast path continues right along the cliffs (there is reasonable access to the beach), take the left fork and climb steeply up below the lookout to reach the wall in front of **Gara Rock Hotel**.

6 Turn left to reach the hotel drive and walk straight on up the lane. After 100yds (91m) turn left through a gate in the hedge signposted **'Mill Bay'**. Walk straight across the field (the roped-off area indicates a car park for the beach) with lovely views to Salcombe and Malborough church beyond. Go through a **small copse**, then a gate and across the farm track. Go through a gate.

7 This leads down a beautiful **bridle path**, running gradually downhill beneath huge, ancient pollarded lime trees, with a

what to look for

Many stretches of the coast path are resplendent with wild flowers virtually all the year round, and during the summer months the path below Portlemouth Down is incredible. There are banks of purple wild thyme, heather, gorse, red campion, bladder campion, tiny yellow tormentil and pretty blue scabious. Look out too for the common dodder, a parasitic plant with pretty clusters of pink flowers. It draws the life out of its host plant, often heather or gorse, via suckers.

grassy combe to the right. The path leads past the car park to reach **Mill Bay**.

8 Turn right along the lane. If you want to avoid the steps, look out for a **footpath sign** pointing right, up a narrow, steep, path to regain **East Portlemouth** and your car; if not, continue along the lane and retrace your steps up the steep tarmac path.

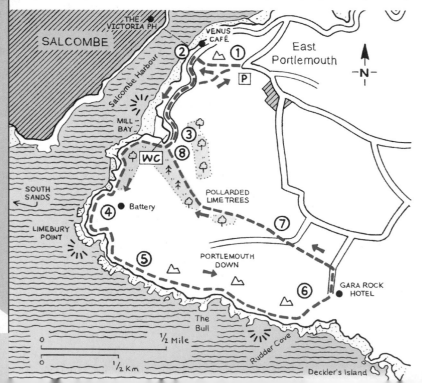

Victoria Inn

Standing on Salcombe's main street, with stunning views across Salcombe Estuary from the smartly refurbished lounge and dining areas, the Victoria is not a typical seaside town pub. Beyond the plain exterior is a super flagstoned bar area, filled with chunky wooden tables and chairs and featuring a log fire and attractive pictures of old Salcombe, and stairs lead up to the civilised lounge bar and restaurant. A great place to end up after this coastal stroll, for a refreshing pint of St Austell ale and a relaxing meal.

Food

Food is freshly prepared from Devon produce and includes fresh fish, local butcher meats and locally made cheeses. Expect decent sandwiches (served with chips), hot leek tart with smoked bacon, smoked haddock mornay, honey-roast ham, eggs and chips, shellfish chowder, and scallops with garlic and parsley butter.

Family facilities

Children are welcome throughout the bars. There's a children's menu in the bar, baby-changing facilities and a play area in the large sheltered terraced garden.

Alternative refreshment stops

Salcombe has pubs, cafés and restaurants, but if you want to stay on the other side try the Venus Café. It's by the ferry slipway, with a pretty garden looking across the water (open March to October).

☞ Where to go from here

Once you've caught the ferry to the other side, you can explore the pretty little town of Salcombe. The ferry runs every day from 8am–7pm on weekdays and from 8.30am–7pm on weekends and bank holidays. You can see chocolates being made at the Salcombe Chocolate Factory (www.salcombe.co.uk) and enjoy a visit to an exotic coastal garden and a house displaying toys, dolls and a natural history collection – Overbecks Museum and Garden at Sharpitor.

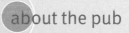

about the pub

Victoria Inn

Fore Street, Salcombe
Devon TQ8 8BU
Tel 01548 842604
www.victoriasalcombe.com

DIRECTIONS: on Salcombe's main street	
PARKING: none (public car park opposite)	
OPEN: daily; all day	
FOOD: daily	
BREWERY/COMPANY: St Austell Brewery	
REAL ALE: St Austell Tinners Ale, Dartmoor Best, HSD and Tribute Ale	
DOGS: allowed in the bar	

Woods around Lustleigh

A relatively gentle way through Lustleigh Cleave – through Wreyland's old, thatched farmhouses, the unspoilt village of Lustleigh and steeply back uphill.

Lustleigh – A traditional village

Lustleigh is one of those perfect Devon villages that everyone just has to see. The rose-covered cottages and pub cluster tightly around the green and 13th-century Church of St John the Baptist. The quintessentially English cricket field, rushing streams and boulder-strewn hill slopes, all nestling together in a deep wooded valley beneath the eastern fringe of Dartmoor, make this a real magnet. But Lustleigh has a problem of no central car park, although there is now one as you enter the village from the A382. Many people weave their way through the cars parked on narrow lanes around the church and drive off again in frustration. But there is another way of getting a feel for the real Lustleigh: drive on through the village, park and walk back in.

Lustleigh still holds a traditional May Day ceremony, which takes place on the first Saturday in May. The festival had died out, but was revived in the early years of the 20th century by Cecil Torr who,

while living at Wreyland, wrote his famous three-volume work *Small Talk at Wreyland*, a charming record of rural life. The crowning ceremony at that time took place at Long Tor on the outskirts of the village. The May Queen, dressed in white and garlanded with spring flowers (and elected from the local children – candidates must have danced around the maypole on at least five previous occasions) leads a procession around the village beneath a canopy of flowers which is held aloft by other Lustleigh children. She is then crowned on the May Day rock in the Town Orchard. A new granite throne was set in place on the rock to celebrate the Millennium, and the names of recent May Queens are carved below.

the walk

1 Walk back along the lane towards Lustleigh. Pass **Waye Farm**, and shortly after turn right up a stony track signed 'Lustleigh Cleave'. Pass through **Heaven's Gate** and proceed downhill into the valley. Turn left through a gate into **Woodland Trust** land. Follow grassy paths to a track at the bottom of the hill.

2 Turn left through conifers, past the ivy-covered ruins of **Boveycombe Farm**, to reach a fork. Go right towards the old packhorse bridge at **Hisley**. Don't cross over; turn left and follow the river bank into the **Bovey Valley Woodlands**. Keep along the river bank, pass through a gate and across the field to join a lane at a metal gate.

Left: A field above Lustleigh village

2h00 — **4 MILES** — **6.4 KM** — **LEVEL 1 2 3**

WALK

MAP: OS Explorer OL28 Dartmoor
START/FINISH: by side of lane at Hammerslake, grid ref: SX 774815
PATHS: tracks through woodland, over fields and along steep, narrow country lanes
LANDSCAPE: steep, wooded valley, farmland, thatched cottages and village
PUBLIC TOILETS: in village
TOURIST INFORMATION: Bovey Tracey, tel 01626 832047
THE PUB: The Cleave, Lustleigh
❶ Some steep ascents and descents on rough paths and lanes are not suitable for very young children

Getting to the start
Lustleigh is off the A382 between Moretonhampstead and Bovey Tracey, 4 miles (6.4km) north west of Bovey Tracey. At the war memorial, follow the road left to the church and then turn left, following the signs for Rudge. Turn right at Rudge Cross, signposted to Pethybridge. Keep straight on, passing two roads dropping to the left. The road soon widens where there are railings to the right and there are a few short areas to pull in close to the left of the road.

Researched and written by:
Brian Pearse, Sue Viccars

Lustleigh DEVON

WALK

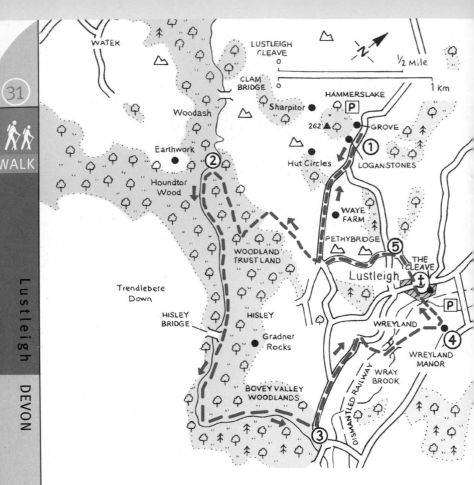

3 Turn left uphill and take the first lane right. Soon take the footpath signed **'Wreyland'** right. Keep right, following the path to cross the bridge over **Wray Brook**. Go left (note the old railway viaduct on the left) and follow the signs along the field edge then through a gate into Wreyland.

4 Turn left to pass **Wreyland Manor** (dating from the 1360s, but altered in 1680) and cricket pitch and enter **Lustleigh** by the green, the oldest part, with its stone cross erected in memory of Henry Tudor, rector 1888–1904. Turn left at the church and go straight ahead between the dairy

and post office into the Town Orchard. Carry on past the **May Day rock** to the end of the orchard and cross the leat on a wooden bridge. Go through the gate and, at the next junction of paths, drop down right to see the **magical granite 'footbridge'**.

5 Retrace your steps to the junction and go straight over to join the lane. Turn left, then first right to zig-zag very steeply up a lane to **Pethybridge**, between two thatched cottages. Turn left, then right at the top. Walk past **Waye Farm** and return to your car.

The Cleave

about the pub

The Cleave
Lustleigh, Bovey Tracey
Devon TQ13 9TJ
Tel 01647 277223
www.thecleave.com

DIRECTIONS: see Getting to the start; pub in village centre

PARKING: 8 (use village car park)

OPEN: closed Monday October to March

FOOD: daily

BREWERY/COMPANY: Heavitree

REAL ALE: Flowers Original, Bass, Wadworth 6X, Otter Ale

DOGS: allowed inside

Originally a Devon longhouse, this 15th-century thatched inn, on Dartmoor's eastern flanks, is a perfect pit-stop for walkers. It appeared in the 1939 film Hound of the Baskervilles, and was the unofficial waiting-room for the now long-gone railway station. The cosy lounge bar has granite walls, high-backed settles and a vast inglenook fireplace with crackling winter log fire. The bigger Victorian bar has a larger dresser, attractive prints and an impressive collection of musical instruments. In summer, head for the very pretty sheltered garden, replete with colourful hanging baskets and borders.

Food
Menu includes baked local trout, pheasant braised with bacon, shallots, mushrooms and Madeira, home-made steak, kidney and ale pie, roast beef and Yorkshire pudding, and grilled belly pork. At lunchtime expect soups, patés and ploughman's.

Family facilities
Children of all ages are welcome inside the pub. There's a family room with books, crayons and games, smaller portions of main meals are available, and you'll find high chairs and baby-changing facilities.

Alternative refreshment stops
The Primrose Cottage Tearooms provide the perfect setting for a Devon cream tea.

☛ Where to go from here
Becka Falls are just south of Manaton on the Bovey Tracey road. This natural waterfall, where the Becka Brook tumbles more than 80ft (24m) over a succession of huge granite boulders, is at its most impressive after heavy rainfall (www.beckafalls-dartmoor.com). Visit the House of Marbles in Bovey Tracey and watch the skilled craftsmen blowing paperweights and shaping glass. There are also three museums explaining the history of the Bovey Potteries, glass, board games and marbles (www.houseofmarbles.com).

Along the Dart Valley trail

32

🚲
CYCLE

Dart Valley

DEVON

The Dart Valley Trail

Cycle through woods and parkland above the tranquil River Dart south of the historic town of Totnes.

Totnes and Ashprington

The River Dart at Totnes – today a focus for tourists and pleasure craft – has always played an important part in the fortunes of the town. At the lowest crossing point of the river, the first stone bridge was built in the early 13th century. By Tudor times Totnes was Devon's second most important port, heavily involved in the woollen industry, and also exporting tin and granite from Dartmoor's mines. Even back in the 10th century there was a Saxon burgh here; later the Normans made their mark by building the motte-and-bailey castle that dominates the town even today. From the motte you can clearly see the structure of the town, the original parts of which were walled in the 12th century. Totnes still has many fine 15th- and 16th-century buildings.

When you cycle downhill into Ashprington you feel as if you've entered something of a time warp. This pretty village, nestling in the folds of the hills, was originally part of the Sharpham Estate, though many of the buildings were sold off in 1940. Despite this most retain the characteristic lattice

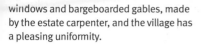

windows and bargeboarded gables, made by the estate carpenter, and the village has a pleasing uniformity.

the ride

1 From the car park follow the road back towards Totnes. Turn left onto Seymour Road, then left over **Totnes Bridge** (built to replace a smaller one in 1838, and a toll bridge until 1881) – the lowest crossing point of the Dart – to reach the roundabout at the bottom of Fore Street. Turn left along **The Plains**, at one time an area of tidal marsh; the old riverside warehouses have now been converted into stylish accommodation. Keep ahead along New Walk to reach the **Steam Packet Inn** on the left.

2 As the road bends sharp left turn right up narrow tarmac **Moat Hill**. After about 20yds (18m) turn left as signed 'Ashprington' on a gritty, fenced track, gently uphill.

3 At the end bear right then left onto the old driveway to **Sharpham House**, initially walled. Pass out into the open briefly – look back for good views over the river at Totnes – then back into woodland. Continue uphill to cross a cattle grid in woodland. There follows a lovely downhill run through parkland, with fantastic views ahead left over reedbeds fringing the river. The drive runs uphill into woodland again and passes into the **Sharpham Estate** via a gate. Continue through two more gates and back into parkland – watch out for cowpats beneath your wheels and cows in front of you! A long downhill run, with **Linhay Plantation** right, leads towards the river. Pass through a gate on a track to reach a signpost.

2h00 | **7 MILES** | **11.3 KM** | **LEVEL 123**

CYCLE

Dart Valley

DEVON

MAP: OS Explorer OL20 South Devon
START/FINISH: Steamer Quay (or Longmarsh) car park, grid ref: SX 809596
TRAILS/TRACKS: country house drive, rough woodland path, tarmac lane
LANDSCAPE: river valley, parkland, rolling woods and farmland
PUBLIC TOILETS: Steamer Quay, Totnes
TOURIST INFORMATION: Totnes, tel 01803 863168
CYCLE HIRE: B R Trott Cycle Hire, Warland Garage, Totnes, tel 01803 862493
THE PUB: The Durant Arms, Ashprington
🔴 Steep ascent/descent through woodland near Ashprington: cyclists should dismount

Getting to the start

Totnes lies on the A385 between the A38 and Torbay. Follow signs for the Steamer Quay from the bottom of Fore Street. If Steamer Quay is full, keep ahead to Longmarsh overflow car park.

Why do this cycle ride?

The ideal escape route from the hustle and bustle of Totnes – which can get very busy in holiday times – to the peaceful, beautiful valley of the River Dart. The ride undulates through parkland and meadows of the Sharpham Estate, overlooking the meandering Dart, before a tough climb through woodland. The delightful village of Ashprington, and The Durant Arms provide a great – and welcome! – focus.

Researched and written by. Sue Viccars

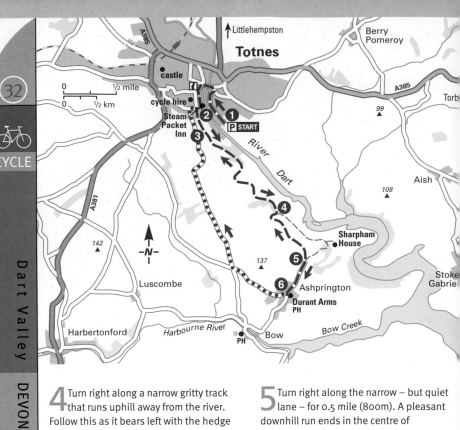

4 Turn right along a narrow gritty track that runs uphill away from the river. Follow this as it bears left with the hedge and continues uphill. Pass over a **cattle grid**, at which point cyclists are asked to dismount. Continue up the rough, rooty track – Leafy Lane – through **Lower Gribble Plantation** – it's quite a slog. Pass through a staggered barrier; the track levels off and reaches a lane, with the entrance to **Sharpham House** left. Sharpham House was built in the late 18th century – replacing an Elizabethan building – for Captain Philemon Pownall of HMS *Favourite*, funded by prize money from the capture of a Spanish treasure ship. His grandson later lost Sharpham when he gambled away the family fortune. Situated on the warm south-facing slopes above the Dart, the estate now hosts a working vineyard and cheese dairy, and has a shop and café – definitely worth a visit.

5 Turn right along the narrow – but quiet lane – for 0.5 mile (800m). A pleasant downhill run ends in the centre of Ashprington. **The Durant Arms** – an inn since 1725 and renamed in honour of the Durant family of Sharpham – will be found on the left.

6 To return to Totnes, it would be possible to follow a different route along the undulating country lanes. Turn right at the **war memorial** in Ashprington and follow the lane to Ashprington Cross. Turn right and follow that lane all the way back to meet **Moat Hill**; turn right for New Walk. However, Devon lanes are usually narrow and twisty, with high hedges and poor visibility; it's far safer to return by the outward route (which has lovely views north towards Dartmoor).

The Durant Arms

about the pub

The Durant Arms
Ashprington, Totnes
Devon TQ9 7UP
Tel 01803 732240
www.thedurantarms.com

DIRECTIONS: village is signposted off the A381 south of Totnes; pub in the square	
PARKING: 7 (+ street parking)	
OPEN: daily	
FOOD: daily	
BREWERY/COMPANY: free house	
REAL ALE: St Austell Tribute and Dartmoor Best	
ROOMS: 8 en suite	

Off the tourist trail in the popular South Hams and situated in the heart of a sleepy village, this neat and tidy, cream-painted 18th-century pub has developed a local clientele, who favour the honest home-cooked food that can be enjoyed here. A flagged entrance hall leads into the beamed, open-plan bar, with a popular window seat overlooking the village street, and into the spick-and-span dining rooms, adorned with oils and watercolours by local artists. A small terraced garden with hardwood furniture and a water feature makes a pleasant alternative to the bar in warm weather.

Food

Very good food using fresh local produce ranges from steak and kidney pie and ham, egg and chips to sirloin steak and a blackboard listing the day's fresh fish, where you may find skate, halibut, lemon sole, and scallops and tiger prawns in cream and white wine sauce. Sandwiches are available at lunchtime.

Family facilities

There's a separate children's area away from the bar and they are welcome inside if eating. A children's menu and half-portions of some main menu dishes are available, as are high chairs. No children overnight.

Alternative refreshment stops

There's a good choice of cafés and pubs, including the Steam Packet Inn in Totnes, and there's a café at Sharpham Vineyard.

👉 Where to go from here

Enjoy a stream train trip through the lovely, unspoilt scenery of the wooded Dart Valley from Totnes to Buckfastleigh on the South Devon Railway (www.southdevonrailway.org). Take a cruise along the River Dart to Dartmouth (www.riverlink.co.uk), explore the streets of Totnes and visit the town's castle, one of the best surviving examples of a Norman motte-and-bailey castle (www.english-heritage.org.uk). Attractions near Newton Abbot include the Devon Bird of Prey Centre (www.devonbirdofprey.co.uk), and the Hedgehog Hospital and British Wildlife Garden Centre (www.hedgehog.org.uk), while Torquay offers a wealth of things to see and do, including Babbacombe Model Village (www.babbacombemodelvillage.co.uk), Kent's Cavern (www.kent-cavern.co.uk), and Living Coasts which explores coastlines around the world without leaving Torquay (www.livingcoasts.org.uk).

Bridford and the Teign Valley

Daffodils at Steps Bridge, a climb up Heltor Rock on route for Bridford and a very special church.

Teign Valley

In early springtime many people travel out to Steps Bridge (built in 1816) to stroll along the River Teign, enjoying the sight of thousands of tiny wild daffodils crowding the riverbanks. But there's a better way to explore this valley, which includes a close look at an example of that most characteristic Dartmoor feature, a tor, and a pint at one of the Teign Valley's best pubs as an added bonus!

Much of the ancient semi-natural woodland and valley meadows around Steps Bridge is a Site of Special Scientific Interest (SSSI), and many acres are owned by the National Trust. Dunsford Wood (on the opposite bank of the Teign from the car park) is managed as a nature reserve by the Devon Wildlife Trust. These woodlands are glorious all year round: there are snowdrops in February, daffodils in early spring, wood anemones and ransoms; then foxgloves, woodrush and cow-wheat in summer. Look out for the nests of the wood ant by the side of the path, which can be as much as a metre high. If you place your cheek or hand near to a nest you'll get a shock – the ants squirt formic acid from their abdomens in a defensive move, and it stings!

Blackingstone Rock is another outlying tor, 1 mile (1.6km) south west of Heltor Rock. Turn right rather than left at Point 4 and you will soon be aware of its huge, granite mass rising above the lane on the left. You can get to the top by climbing up an almost vertical flight of steps which was added in the 19th century for that purpose. The views of the surrounding countryside are worth the effort.

While you're in Bridford, part way round the walk, it's well worthwhile going inside the church. The original chapel on this site was dedicated by Bishop Bronescombe in 1259, to the murdered Archbishop Thomas á Becket, who died at Canterbury Cathedral in 1170. This was still a common practice in many West Country churches during the century following his death. The present building dates from the 15th century, and its most famous feature is the superb eight-bay rood screen, thought to date from 1508. The faces of the richly carved and coloured figures were mutilated by Puritan soldiers during the Civil War, but what survives is still impressive. The doors are also unusual in that they are made in one piece rather than being divided in the middle. These details are often overlooked by the Steps Bridge hordes.

the walk

1 Cross the road, following the signs to the **youth hostel**. Turn right up the concrete track, then left. When you reach the youth hostel turn right again, this time following signs for **Heltor Farm**. The steep path leads uphill through delightful oak, then beech woodland. At a fork of paths turn left and up over some wooden steps by the gate into a field.

2 Follow wooden footpath posts straight up the field. Go through the metal gate, then between granite gateposts; look right to see **Heltor Rock**. Pass signs for **Lower Heltor Farm**. Before a metal gate onto a green lane, turn left through a wooden

gate following permissive footpath signs through a new woodland. With a dog you may need to continue on the Right of Way around the farmhouse.

3 Follow the signs down wooden steps, across **ponds** and through a gate. Turn left up the tarmac lane.

4 At the top of the lane turn left (signs for **Bridford**). After 200yds (183m) turn left over a stile up the narrow fenced permissive path to **Heltor,** from where you can enjoy an amazing panorama. Retrace your steps to the road and turn left.

5 The lane eventually bends left, then right, to reach the edge of **Bridford**. Turn right down a small steep lane signed 'Parish Hall and Church'. Follow the path round the churchyard, down steps and right to find **The Bridford Inn**.

The River Teign at Steps Bridge in Bridford Woods

2h45 — **5 MILES** — **8 KM** — **LEVEL 1 2 3**

MAP: OS Explorer 110 Torquay & Dawlish

START/FINISH: free car park at Steps Bridge, grid ref: SX 804883

PATHS: woodland paths, open fields and country lanes, 7 stiles

LANDSCAPE: steeply wooded valleys and undulating farmland

PUBLIC TOILETS: at car park

TOURIST INFORMATION: Moretonhampstead, tel 01647 440043

THE PUB: The Bridford Inn, Bridford

🚫 Some steep woodland paths

Getting to the start

Steps Bridge is on the B3212 between Exeter and Moretonhampstead, 9 miles (14.4km) west of Exeter. Steps Bridge is not long after the signs for Dunsford and is well signposted itself. Cross the bridge and go a little up the hill, past the Steps Bridge Café and turn right into the car park.

Researched and written by: Brian Pearse, Sue Viccars

6 Turn left from the pub and follow the road through the centre of the village. Take the fourth lane (**Neadon Lane**) on the right, by a telephone box. Just past where a bridleway joins (from the left) the lane dips to the right, downhill; take the left fork ahead to pass **Birch Down Farm**. Take the path up to the left, beside the field behind the farm. Take the stile and cross the field, keeping the wire fence to your right. Continue up the right-hand edge of the next field to a stile in the top corner. Then cross over a **tumbledown granite wall** and carry straight on through an area of prickly gorse bushes, heading towards a footpath signpost. Cross a stile by some beech trees.

7 Continue along the top of the field and down a green lane towards **Lower Lowton Farm**. At a wooden gate turn right along the permissive bridleway to avoid the farm. At the next T-junction turn right, towards **Steps Bridge**, then through a small wooden gate. Continue down the deeply banked green lane until you reach a gate onto a surfaced lane.

8 Turn left through the middle gate, signed **'Byway to Steps Bridge'**. At the edge of **Bridford Wood** (by the National Trust sign) turn right following the footpath signposts. The path is fairly narrow and quite steep. Go left, then right, to cross a sandy track, keeping downhill. The path then runs to the left, now high above the river to **Steps Bridge** where it meets the road opposite the café. Turn left here to return to your car.

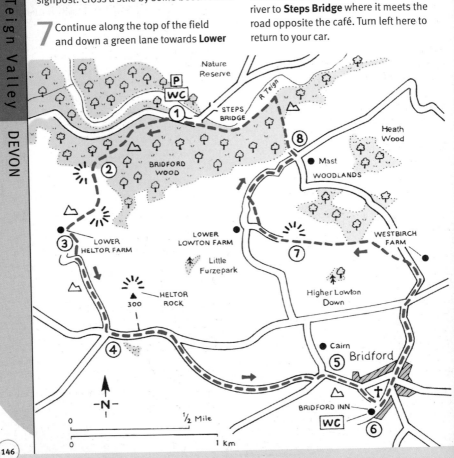

The Bridford Inn

Deep down twisting narrow lanes on the edge of the Dartmoor National Park, the Bridford Inn appropriately advertises itself as being 'the middle of nowhere, the centre of the universe'. It can be found at the end of the village and is a cracking community local with a popular games room replete with dart board and pool table. Speciality evenings, great bar food and locally-brewed beers draw locals and walkers into the big bar with its blazing winter log fire and warm welcome.

Food

Expect traditional pub meals in the form of lunchtime sandwiches, lasagne, cod and chips, various basket meals, and home-made soups, steak and ale pie, ham, egg and chips, and Sunday roast lunches.

Family facilities

Children are welcome inside and youngsters have their own menu to choose from. The beer garden has a play area.

Alternative refreshment stops

Another good pub just down the road is the Royal Oak at Dunsford. The Steps Bridge Café is open 10am–6pm and offers accommodation.

☛ Where to go from here

Go and have a look at the three reservoirs near Hennock, on the ridge between the Teign and Wray valleys – Tottiford, Kennick and Trenchford. These beautiful expanses of fresh water, surrounded by coniferous woodland and rhododendron-covered slopes, provide plentiful opportunities for easy walks and peaceful picnics. Head south through the Teign Valley to view the Canonteign Falls, a magical combination of waterfalls, woodlands and lakes. To the north is the impressive Castle Drogo, a granite castle built between 1910 and 1930 by Sir Edwin Lutyens, and which combines the grandeur of a medieval castle with the comfort of a 20th-century home (www.nationaltrust.org.uk).

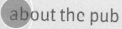

about the pub

The Bridford Inn
Bridford, Moretonhampstead
Devon EX6 7HT
Tel: 01647 256436

DIRECTIONS: village signposted off the B3212 at Dunsford; Point **6** on walk	
PARKING: 24	
OPEN: closed Tuesday lunchtime	
FOOD: daily	
BREWERY/COMPANY: free house	
REAL ALE: Teign Valley Bitter, guest beers	
DOGS: allowed inside	

Along cliffs to Dartmouth Castle

An easy round along the cliffs to Blackstone Point and Dartmouth Castle – and a ferry ride to the pub.

Dartmouth

Dartmouth seems to have everything. The town has a rich and illustrious history and occupies a commanding position on the banks of the Dart. It developed as a thriving port and shipbuilding town from the 12th century. By the 14th century it enjoyed a flourishing wine trade, and benefited from the profits of piracy for generations. Today pleasure craft and the tourist industry have taken over in a big way but Dartmouth has lost none of its charm.

Now cared for by English Heritage, 15th-century Dartmouth Castle enjoys a beautiful position at the mouth of the Dart. It was one of the most advanced fortresses of the day and, with Kingswear Castle opposite, was built to protect the homes and warehouses of the town's merchants.

Visitors experience a representation of life in the later Victorian gun battery that was established. A record of 1192 infers that there was a monastic foundation on the site, leading to the establishment of St Petrock's Church, rebuilt in Gothic style within the castle precincts in 1641.

The cobbled quayside at Bayard's Cove, with its attractive and prosperous 17th- and 18th-century buildings) was used during filming of the 1970s' BBC TV series *The Onedin Line*. The single-storey artillery fort at Bayard's Cove was built before 1534 to protect the harbour. You can see the gunports at ground level and the remains of stairs leading to a walled walk. A plaque commemorates the sailing of the *Mayflower* and *Speedwell* from the quay in 1620.

the walk

1 Go through the right-hand car park, following the signs '**Coast Path Dartmouth**'. Continue through a kissing gate, keeping the hedge to your right.

Left: Willow Cove
Below: Deadmans Cove

Walk through the next field, then through a gate to join the **coast path**.

2 Turn left; there are lovely views here west to Start Point and east towards the Day Beacon above Kingswear. The coast path runs a little inland from the cliff edge, but you can always go straight ahead to walk above **Warren Point** (a plaque reveals that the Devon Federation of Women's Institutes gave this land to the National Trust in 1970).

3 Continue left to pass above **Western Combe Cove** (with steps down to the sea) and then **Combe Point** (take care – it's a long drop to the sea from here).

4 Rejoin the coast path through an open gateway in a wall and follow it above **Shinglehill Cove**. The path turns inland, passes through a gate, becomes narrow and a little overgrown, and twists along the back of **Willow Cove**. It passes through a wooded section (with a field on the left) and then climbs around the back of Compass Cove. Keep going to pass through a gate. Keep left to reach a wooden footpath post, then turn sharp right, down the valley to the cliff edge. Follow the path on, through a gate near **Blackstone Point**.

5 Leave the path right to clamber down onto the rocks here – you get a superb view over the mouth of the estuary. Retrace your steps and continue on the **coast path** as it turns inland along the side of the estuary and runs through deciduous woodland.

| 2h00 | 3 MILES | 4.8 KM | LEVEL 123 |

MAP: OS Explorer OL20 South Devon
START/FINISH: National Trust car parks at Little Dartmouth, grid ref: SX 874491
PATHS: easy coastal footpath and green lanes
LANDSCAPE: farmland, cliff tops and river estuary
PUBLIC TOILETS: Dartmouth Castle
TOURIST INFORMATION: Dartmouth, tel 01803 834224
THE PUB: Royal Castle Hotel, Dartmouth
⚠ Generally easy but care to be taken with children along the clifftop paths

Getting to the start

Little Dartmouth is about 2 miles (3.2km) south of Dartmouth on the A379. On the outskirts of Dartmouth (A3122) from Totnes, turn right along the A379 towards Stoke Fleming. Turn left in a mile (1.6km), signposted to Little Dartmouth Farm, keep ahead at the next crossroads, following signs for the farm. At the next junction turn left for one of the National Trust car parks.

Researched and written by:
Brian Pearse, Sue Viccars

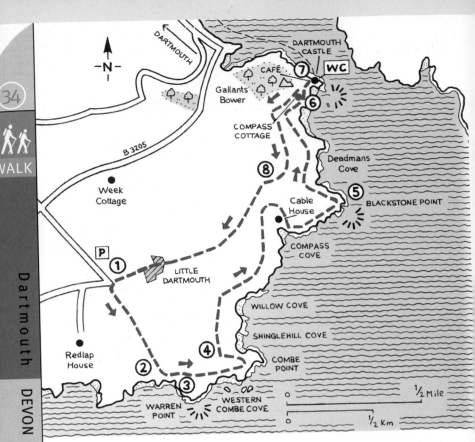

6 The path meets a surfaced lane opposite **Compass Cottage**; go right onto the lane and immediately right again steeply downhill, keeping the wall to your left. At the turning space go right down steps to reach the **castle** and café.

7 Retrace your route up the steps to the tarmac lane at Point 6, then left to pass Compass Cottage, and straight on up the steep lane (signposted '**Little Dartmouth**') and through a kissing gate onto National Trust land.

8 The path runs along the top of a field and through a five-bar gate onto a green lane. Go through a gate and the

farmyard at Little Dartmouth and ahead on a tarmac lane to the **car park**.

what to look for

Dartmouth, both on shore and on the water, is always buzzing with activity – it never stops. There's masses to watch including pleasure steamers, private cruisers, brightly coloured dinghies, rowing boats, ferries, expensive ocean-going yachts, canoeists and even huge cruise ships, calling in for a night en route for sunnier climes. You'll also notice naval craft, ranging from old-fashioned whalers to modern frigates which are connected with the Britannia Royal Naval College, which overlooks the town. Princes Charles and Andrew both studied here.

Royal Castle Hotel

Commanding the best site overlooking the small harbour and the Dart estuary beyond, this handsome inn is a most welcoming and comfortable place to stay. Originally four Tudor houses built on either side of a narrow lane, which now forms the lofty and attractive hallway, it boasts antique furniture and the magnificent Bell Board, full of room-call bells. Of the two bars, the Harbour Bar is distinctively pubby and lively throughout the day, with local farm cider and cask ales on tap. The more refined and spacious Galleon Bar is a popular coffee stop. Tudor fireplaces, spiral staircases, priest holes and period furniture all contribute to the sense of history.

Food
Bar food ranges from filled jacket potatoes, ploughman's, salads and sandwiches, to whole plaice, local sausages, mash and onion gravy, scallops and mushroom risotto, and chargrilled rib-eye steak with mushroom sauce. The upstairs restaurant specialises in local seafood, including lobster, crab, Dover Sole and, perhaps, oven-roasted sea bass with almond butter.

Family facilities
Young children are welcome overnight (3 family rooms) and in the restaurant (high chairs, smaller portions), but under 14s are not allowed in the bars.

Alternative refreshment stops
There's the Castle Tearooms at Dartmouth Castle and masses of very good eating places in Dartmouth – including the best prawn sandwiches, available from a shop on the right past the lower ferry slipway.

about the pub

Royal Castle Hotel
11 The Quay, Dartmouth
Devon TQ6 9PS
Tel 01803 833033
www.royalcastle.co.uk

DIRECTIONS: catch the ferry or follow the B3205 into the town centre, the hotel is on The Quay close to good parking areas
PARKING: 14 (use town car parks)
OPEN: daily; all day
FOOD: daily; all day
BREWERY/COMPANY: free house
REAL ALE: Bass, Dobbs Bitter, Courage Directors
DOGS: allowed in the bars
ROOMS: 25 en suite

☞ Where to go from here
Drive into Dartmouth or catch the ferry from Stumpy Steps (just upriver from the castle), which within a few minutes will deposit you right in the centre of Dartmouth where you can explore the town's streets, quay and the fascinating museum in Duke Street. The ferry saves you a further mile (1.6km) walk and there's a continuous shuttle service from the castle from 10.15am until 5pm. Cross the Dart by ferry to Kingswear and take a trip on the Paignton and Dartmouth Steam Railway (www.paignton-steamrailway.co.uk). West of Dartmouth at Blackawton is Woodlands, a 60-acre site packed with exhilarating rides and indoor and outdoor attractions (www.woodlandspark.com).

Exeter Ship Canal

Follow the banks of the historic Exeter Ship Canal from the heart of the city to the Turf Lock, where the canal rejoins the Exe estuary.

Exeter

Quite apart from the old quayside, there's much to explore in Exeter itself. There has been a settlement here, at the lowest crossing point of the Exe, since before the Romans established Isca Dumnoniorum (named after the local tribe) in AD 50. The settlement marked the western limit of Roman occupation of the south-west, and about two thirds of the Roman city walls are still visible today. In the 1970s the magnificent Roman bathhouse was excavated, and now lies protected beneath paving slabs outside the West Front of the Norman Cathedral Church of St Peter. Largely built of Beer stone, quarried from the cliffs of east Devon, the cathedral's intricately carved West Front is stunning. The twin towers survived an extensive rebuild from 1270 to1360.

Exeter has a wealth of medieval churches, and the Cathedral Close has some good examples of Tudor and Stuart architecture, which miraculously escaped significant bomb damage in May 1942. The 16th-century Ship Inn in St Martin's Lane is reputed to have been visited by Sir Francis Drake, and black-and-white timbered Mol's Coffee House on the corner of The Close also dates from that time.

the ride

1 From Saddles & Paddles cross the quay to the riverside. Turn right and cycle upstream to **Cricklepit Bridge** (built in 1905); turn right over the bridge, and right again on the other side. Cycle along the broad **riverside walkway**, passing Bar Venezia and Roger's Tearoom on the right. Keep ahead to cycle between the river on the left and canal basin (originally called The New Cut) on the right, built in 1830 to extend ship accommodation at the Exeter end of the canal. Pass **Trew's Weir**, and the **Port Royal** on the opposite bank, to reach the canal (Welcome Inn ahead right).

Cycling on the Exe Valley Way, part of the Exeter Ship Canal

Storm clouds over the canal basin

2h15 — **12 MILES** — **19.3 KM** — **LEVEL 1**23

2 Turn left over the canal; turn right along the tarmac way between the canal and the flood prevention 'trough'. Where the path forks, keep left. Look for yellow flag iris and purple loosestrife below left. Pass **playing fields** on the right, bearing right at the end to reach the canal by a small car park (right).

3 Do not cross the canal; turn left on a **tarmac cycle track** that parallels the canal. The track bears away from the canal to pass to the left of the Double Locks pub, built in 1702. Continue on to a fork just before the A379, passing the **Double Locks Wetlands** on the left, a managed area of reedbeds, a haven for wildflowers, dragonflies, birds and insects.

4 Take the right fork; cross the A379 at the **traffic lights** (note the swing bridge over the canal). On the other side, the track becomes (initially) narrower and rougher. Pass a small parking area (right), then cycle under the M5; from now on you're out in peaceful countryside. The Exe Estuary silted up during the 14th century, and the canal – the earliest working ship canal in England – was started around 1564, linking Exeter to Trenchard's Sluice (which entered the river by the M5 viaduct). The canal was extended to Topsham (a port since Roman times, seen across the canal and river to the left) in 1676. In the early 19th century – under the engineer James Green – it reached the Turf Lock. Its fortunes deteriorated after Brunel's railway reached Exeter in 1844, and then Exmouth (on the east side of the estuary) in 1861.

MAP: OS Explorer 114 Exeter & the Exe Valley and 110 Torquay & Dawlish

START/FINISH: The Quay, Exeter, grid ref: SX 920920

TRAILS/TRACKS: well-surfaced path

LANDSCAPE: rural townscape, canal and estuary, marsh

PUBLIC TOILETS: at the start

TOURIST INFORMATION: Exeter, tel 01392 265700

CYCLE HIRE: Saddles and Paddles, The Quay, Exeter, tel 01392 424241

THE PUB: The Turf Hotel, Exminster

🛑 Busy crossing of A379 (but traffic lights for walkers/cyclists)

Getting to the start

Exeter Quay lies on the north side of the River Exe in the old West Quarter. Follow brown tourist signs (with an anchor logo) for the quayside. There is no parking on the quay. Park in the Cathedral and Quay car park, just above The Quay.

Why do this cycle ride?

Exeter has an impressive maritime heritage, and this ride starts and finishes at the very hub: the old quayside. The route runs through a lovely stretch of 'inner city' countryside before striking south along the canal through nature reserves and marshes to reach the Turf Hotel, situated on the Exe estuary.

Researched and written by: Sue Viccars

Exeter   DEVON

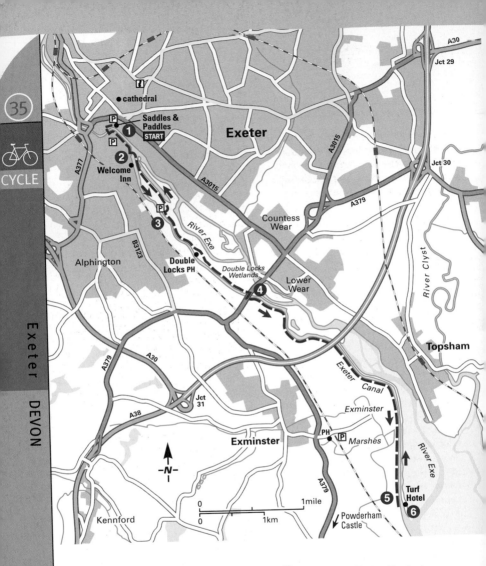

5 Arrive at the basin at the **Turf Lock** (constructed in 1827), where the canal reaches the Exe Estuary and you have lovely views ahead towards the sea. The building housing The Turf Hotel was built around the same time, and probably accommodated visiting boat crews. Horse-drawn barges then transported goods up the canal to Exeter.

6 Cycle back to **Exeter**. Exminster Marshes (this side) and Bowling Green marshes (on the other side of the estuary) are RSPB reserves, so keep an eye out for birdlife. Spring brings lapwing and redshank; through autumn and winter thousands of curlew, wigeon, teal, golden plover and dunlin, for example, come here to feed and roost. It's also important for migrant birds, including elegant avocets.

The Turf Hotel

about the pub

The Turf Hotel
Turf Locks, Exminster
Exeter, Devon EX6 8EE
Tel 01392 833128
www.turfpub.net

DIRECTIONS: the pub cannot be reached by car; nearest parking 0.75 mile (1.2km) up the canal and accessed from the A379 Dawlish road, turning left at the mini-roundabout at the end of the Exminster by-pass

PARKING: none – see above

OPEN: daily; all day June to August; Saturday and Sunday April, May and September; weekends only until 6pm October and March; closed November to February

FOOD: no food Sunday evenings

BREWERY/COMPANY: free house

REAL ALE: Otter Bitter and Bright, Ferryman's Ale

Built around 1830, and remotely situated at the end of Exeter Canal with tranquil views across the Exe estuary and out to sea, the Turf is one of the few pubs in the country that cannot be reached by car.

Arrive by boat, by ferry from Starcross, Topsham or Exeter, by bicycle, or after a 20-minute walk beside the canal. It's worth the effort for the views and the summer cook-your-own barbecue in the huge garden. If the weather is inclement, the simply decorated bar is equally appealing, with its bare board floor, rustic panelled walls, wood-burning stove, eclectic mix of wooden tables and chairs, and bay window-seats with views across the bird-rich mudflats. First-rate Otter beers on hand-pump and local farm cider.

Food

At lunch tuck into sandwiches, filled jacket potatoes, pizzas, shepherd's pie and home-made chilli with taco chips. Evening additions include mussels, Thai chicken curry, sirloin steak and blackboard specials like fresh Exe salmon.

Family facilities

Children are welcome everywhere and they will love playing in the old boat in the garden.

Alternative refreshment stops

The Double Locks pub beside the canal on your route out of Exeter. Plenty of pubs, cafés and restaurants in Exeter.

🐦 Where to go from here

Take a cruise on the Exeter Canal (www.exetercruises.com) or spend some time exploring the city of Exeter, notably St Nicholas Priory, founded in 1087 and featuring a Norman undercroft, a Tudor room and 15th-century kitchen. Enjoy a guided tour of Exeter's most unusual medieval attraction, the atmospheric network of underground passages, built in the 13th century to bring water into the city (www.exeter.gov.uk). Set in beautiful rose gardens and a deer park beside the River Exe, Powderham Castle is the ancestral home of the Earls of Devon.

Bickleigh and the Exe Valley

WALK

Leave the crowds behind at Bickleigh Bridge and explore the lovely Exe Valley.

Bickleigh Mill and Castle

The touristy area round Bickleigh Bridge, 4 miles (6.4km) south of Tiverton, may be too crowded for many people, and you may be tempted to drive straight through to escape the mass of visitors and cars. But dozens of people do stop here to take a picture of the

Bickleigh Cottage Country Hotel, the picturesque thatched building just above the bridge, instantly recognisable from many 'Beautiful Britain' calendars, and which must be one of the most photographed scenes in Devon. But if it's all too much for you there is a quieter side to this part of the Exe Valley, and within a few minutes' walk from the bridge you will feel as if you are miles from anywhere.

Bickleigh Mill, at the beginning of the walk, is a good place to entertain the

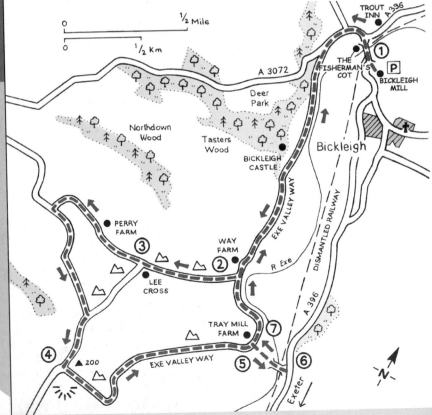

family, with craft, gift and workshops, and a working mill. There's a children's pet area, and the Devon Railway Centre, centred on the Victorian Great Western Railway station, with train rides and model railways. Footpaths lead us to the unspoilt village of Bickleigh, with pretty thatched cottages, the 14th-century church of St Mary the Virgin and a graceful Regency vicarage.

Bickleigh Castle is in a peaceful backwater on the banks of the River Exe. The walk approaches it along a quiet lane, shaded by huge oak, ash and beech trees. An interesting mixture of Norman, medieval and 17th-century architecture, it's a thatched, moated manor house, rather than a castle, and is still lived in. It passed to the de Bickleigh family after the Norman Conquest and was recorded in the Domesday Book. The chapel was built in the 11th century. In the 15th century it belonged to the Courtenays, Earls of Devon, and later to the Carews. Much of the castle was destroyed during the Civil War, and rebuilt in a more homely style. The pink sandstone three-storey gatehouse and moated garden, visible from the lane, are both quite beautiful. There are limited opening hours (the castle is never open on Saturdays) – but it's worth finding out when you can have a proper look round.

the walk

1 From the public parking area at the edge of Bickleigh Mill go back, with care, to the A396 and cross the bridge. Turn left down the A3072, following the brown tourist sign for **Bickleigh Castle**. Take the first lane left, running along the edge of the flood plain on the **Exe Valley Way** (EVW).

2h00	4.25 MILES	6.8 KM	LEVEL 1 2 3

MAP: OS Explorer 114 Exeter & the Exe Valley
START/FINISH: Bickleigh Mill just off A396 at Bickleigh Bridge, grid reference: SX 939075
PATHS: country lanes, one long, steep, muddy track
LANDSCAPE: steeply wooded hillsides and farmland
PUBLIC TOILETS: none on route
TOURIST INFORMATION: Tiverton, tel 01884 255827
THE PUB: The Fisherman's Cot, Bickleigh
⚠ One long, steep and muddy climb

Getting to the start

Bickleigh Mill is 4 miles (6.4km) south of Tiverton and 11 miles (17.7km) north of Exeter on the A396. From Tiverton cross the narrow bridge over the River Exe and turn left immediately into the entrance to Bickleigh Mill. Turn next right along the old railway line and under the bridge to what is signposted as the overflow car park for the mill.

Researched and written by:
Brian Pearse, Sue Viccars

Bickleigh

DEVON

Bickleigh Mill is a converted watermill housing a craft and heritage centre

metal gate onto a concrete standing. Ahead you will see a suspension bridge over the river; cross it and go straight on to reach the dismantled railway track. Do not turn left along the track – although it would take you straight back to your car – it is privately owned and has no public right of way.

Bickleigh Castle will soon be found on the right. Go straight on past **Way Farm**.

2 Just after the buildings of Way Farm turn right to leave the Exe Valley Way, roughly signposted '**Lee Cross & Perry Farm**'. Take care, this is a very narrow lane, carrying busy traffic from local farms. Keep along the lane as it climbs steeply uphill and after 700yds (640m) brings you to the farm at Lee Cross.

3 Immediately after the house keep straight ahead along the road. Pass **Perry Farm** and continue until you reach a T-junction; turn left on to a green lane. Continue on this lane until you reach another T-junction. Turn right. The lane now levels off and becomes easier.

4 Where the green lane meets the tarmac lane turn left and proceed steeply downhill (EVW). The views over the River Exe, and to Silverton church beyond, are glorious. Follow the lane down until you see **Tray Mill Farm** on the right.

5 The way home is straight on along the lane, but it's worth doing a **small detour** to the river here. Turn right through the farmyard (no sign) and pass through a

6 The path goes straight on here to meet the A396. You can do that, turn left, then eventually right to walk through **Bickleigh village** back to the mill, but it is a busy road and you would be better advised to retrace your steps to **Tray Mill Farm** and take the quieter route back to Bickleigh Mill.

7 Back on the lane by Tray Mill Farm, turn right and walk straight along the lane, past Bickleigh Castle, turning right at the A3072, and right again over the bridge to return to your car.

what to look for

Watch the salmon leaping up the weir just below the bridge. This stretch of the Exe is very popular with game fishermen, but the fishing rights are privately owned. Salmon and sea trout fishing licences are available from the Environment Agency, and the season on the Exe runs from mid-February to the end of September. There are strict conservation measures in force to protect spring salmon. The record on the Exe is a fish of over 30lbs (13.6kg) in weight, caught by a man who had never fished for salmon before!

The Fisherman's Cot

about the pub

The Fisherman's Cot
Bickleigh, Tiverton
Devon EX16 8RW
Tel 01884 855237

DIRECTIONS: see Getting to the start; pub by Bickleigh Bridge	
PARKING: 100	
OPEN: daily; all day	
FOOD: daily; all day	
BREWERY/COMPANY: Eldridge Pope	
REAL ALE: Bass, Wadworth 6X	
DOGS: not allowed inside	
ROOMS: 21 en suite	

A rambling, well-appointed thatched inn serving food all day and with a large beer garden beside the fast-flowing River Exe, with good views of the beautiful 16th-century, five-arched Bickleigh Bridge. The open-plan Waterside Bar may not be particularly cosy, but it is the place for snacks and afternoon tea, while the restaurant incorporates a carvery and wide-ranging à la carte menus. Sunday lunch is served, and the champagne and smoked salmon breakfast is optional. The cosy bedrooms are comfortable and well equipped.

Food
From carvery roasts the main menu takes in lunchtime foccacia sandwiches, fish and chips, lasagne and home-made pies.

Family facilities
The pub is geared up for families, offering high chairs and baby-changing facilities, and a children's menu. Please keep children supervised in the riverside garden.

Alternative refreshment stops
The 17th century Trout Inn, just a little upriver, also provides good food and welcomes families. There is a licensed café/bar and restaurant at Bickleigh Mill.

☛ Where to go from here
Take a closer look at the attractions at Bickleigh Mill (www.getlostindevon.co.uk). Head north to Tiverton to explore the 15 galleries at the Museum of Mid Devon Life (www.tivertonmuseum.org.uk), and discover 900 years of history at Tiverton Castle (www.tivertoncastle.com). At

Diggerland near Cullompton, children and adults can drive real diggers

(www.diggerland.com), while at Killerton you can visit Killerton House, an elegant 18th-century house set in an 18-acre (7.3ha) garden with sloping lawns and herbaceous borders (www.nationaltrust.org.uk).

Along the Grand Western Canal to Tiverton

A wonderfully peaceful ride along the banks of the old Grand Western Canal through the GWC Country Park and the beautiful countryside of mid Devon.

Flora & fauna
Disused canals in rural areas provide ideal wildlife habitats, and when you cycle along the Grand Western Canal you certainly feel outnumbered by members of the bird and animal kingdom. This is an ideal site for the water vole – Britain's largest vole, also known as the water rat – whose numbers have fallen drastically in recent years due to a reduction in suitable habitats. There are coots, moorhens and mallards on the water, and robins, starlings, chaffinches and blackbirds around the many picnic spots along the way. You may spot a heron, or a kingfisher by the water.

It's a wonderful place for wildflowers, too: parts of this beautiful reed-fringed canal are carpeted with expanses of white water lilies, harvested until the mid 1960s from a horse-drawn boat. They were laid out at Sampford Peverell wharf, packed and sent around the country to be used in funeral wreaths. You should also see cuckooflower, meadowsweet and yellow loosestrife (uncommon elsewhere in Devon), arrowhead and yellow flag iris rooted in the water's edge, dragonflies, damselflies and butterflies.

the ride

1 From the back of the car park, pass the **tennis court** (left), bear left round a gate and uphill to the tow path (don't go too fast or you might overshoot!). Construction of the canal began in 1810, part of a grand scheme to link the English and Bristol Channels via Exeter and Bristol, but only the Tiverton and Taunton stretch was

Below and right: Canal boats towed along the Grand Western Canal by draught horse

CYCLE

2h15	11 MILES	17.7 KM	LEVEL 1 23

MAP: OS Explorer 128 Taunton & Blackdown Hills and 114 Exeter & the Exe Valley

START/FINISH: Sampford Peverell, grid ref: ST 030142

TRAILS/TRACKS: good canalside path, some stretches grassy, most gritty

LANDSCAPE: canal tow path, farmland, rural townscape

PUBLIC TOILETS: at start and at Tiverton Canal Basin (Point **6**)

TOURIST INFORMATION: Tiverton, tel 01884 255827

CYCLE HIRE: Abbotshood Cycle Hire, Halberton, tel 01884 820728

THE PUB: Globe Inn, Sampford Peverell

❗ Path narrow under bridges - cyclists advised to dismount

Tiverton

DEVON

Getting to the start

Sampford Peverell lies west of M5 junction 27 (Tiverton Parkway). From the M5 follow the A361 Tiverton road; at the first exit (0.5 mile/800m) leave the A361, bear left at the roundabout, and continue into the village. The public car park is signed to the right.

Why do this cycle ride?

The vast majority of visitors to Devon head straight for the coast or moors, and many don't think about exploring the county's heartland. This quiet route along the tow path of the old Grand Western Canal takes you right through the rolling mid-Devon farmland to the centre of Tiverton.

Researched and written by: Sue Viccars

completed. This section – Lowdwells to Tiverton – was completed in 1814. Competition from the railways eventually forced the closure of the canal, although this section was used to transport limestone from quarries around Westleigh to Tiverton as late as 1924.

2 Turn left along the tow path, passing the **Globe Inn**. Pass under **Sampford Peverell bridge** (best to dismount) and continue along a short stretch of quiet lane. Where that bears left, keep ahead along the canalside and you're immediately out in the countryside, with good views of the wooded **Blackdown Hills** to the left – you feel as if you're miles from anywhere. Pass under **Battens Bridge**, then **Rock Bridge**. The next bridge is made of metal. These – look out for them along the route – were originally wooden swing bridges, enabling the passage of barges and linking farmers' land where it was split by the canal.

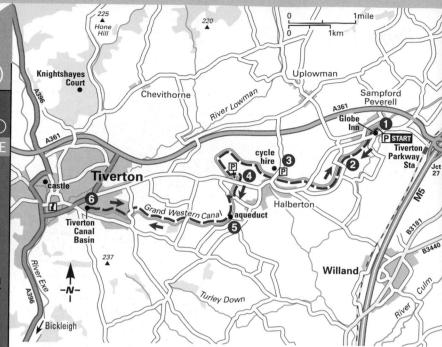

3 Continue along an embanked stretch to pass under Greenway Bridge (car park) and then **Sellake Bridge**. Note how the canal takes a wide sweep (270°) to the left; this is known as the Swan's Neck, and was necessary to avoid the village of Halberton.

4 Next stop is **Tiverton Road Bridge** (car park and picnic area), where you may see canoes and kayaks. There was once a stone-crushing yard here; the journey from a quarry 8 miles (12.9km) away at Whipcott took 2.5 hours, with two horses pulling three 8–10 ton barges. Note milestone III on the left; it's only 3 miles (4.8km) to the basin at Tiverton. Keep on to **Crownhill Bridge**, once known as 'Change Path'. Horses had to change to the right bank here; you do the same by crossing the bridge and turning left.

5 Cross the brick **aqueduct** of the Bristol and Exeter Railway line, built in 1847.

This – the Tiverton branch – closed to passenger traffic in 1964. Three more bridges bring you to neat hedges and bungalows marking the edge of Tiverton. Tidcombe Bridge (look out for milestone I) marks another loop, made necessary by the Bishop of Exeter's refusal to allow the canal within 100yds (91m) of his home (Tidcombe Hall) near by.

6 **Tiverton Canal Basin**, built in 1842, makes an excellent focus for this ride. Refreshments are available at the thatched 16th-century Canal Tearooms, below the basin to the right, or from the floating Barge Canal shop. Look out too for the old lime kilns to the right; limestone was burnt here until the late 19th century to produce fertiliser. Farmers are said to have travelled up to 30 miles (nearly 50km) – each way! – by horse and cart to collect it. To return to **Sampford Peverell**, simply follow the canal tow path back the way you came.

Globe Inn

Handily placed just a mile from the M5 (J27) and beside the Grand Western Canal in a peaceful village, the Globe draws passing travellers and visiting walkers and fishermen exploring the delights of the canal. Beyond the stone and timber façade there's a spacious locals' bar with bare boards, wood-panelled walls and a stone fireplace with a wood-burning stove. The adjoining lounge bar and dining area is carpeted with stone walls and a beamed ceiling. There's also a pretty, flower-decked rear patio with smart tables and chairs and heaters for cool evenings.

about the pub

Globe Inn
16 Lower Town, Sampford Peverell
Tiverton, Devon EX16 7BJ
Tel 01884 821214
www.globe-inn.com

DIRECTIONS: see Getting to the start	
PARKING: 60	
OPEN: daily; all day	
FOOD: daily; all day Friday to Sunday	
BREWERY/COMPANY: Enterprise Inns	
REAL ALE: Greene King Old Speckled Hen, Bass, Otter Bitter	
ROOMS: 6 en suite	

Food

A traditional pub menu takes in a wide range of filled baps and salad platters, standard favourites like haddock and chips, light meals like goat's cheese and tomato tart, and specials like steak, kidney and ale pie and mixed grill. Roast carvery lunches on Sunday.

Family facilities

Children are allowed throughout the pub; there's a children's menu and an excellent play area in the garden.

Alternative refreshment stops

Plenty of choice in Tiverton.

☛ Where to go from here

In Tiverton make time to see the castle, view the 15 galleries at the interesting Museum of Mid Devon Life (www.tivertonmuseum.org.uk), and the town's famous Pannier Market. Cross the M5 to Uffculme to view the Coldharbour Mill Working Wool Museum, which has been producing textiles since 1790. There are machine demonstrations, a water wheel and steam engines (www.coldharbourmill.org.uk). Visit Bickleigh Castle, a fortified manor house that boasts a fascinating history. The restored gatehouse, the ancient chapel and the cob and thatch farmhouse can all be visited (www.bickleighcastle.com).

Exmouth to Knowle

Explore the old Exmouth to Budleigh Salterton railway line with the chance of a stop at the pub in Knowle.

The Jurassic Coast

No visit to this part of Devon would be complete without a visit to the coast, and that's one thing that's missing from this cycle ride. Go down to Exmouth's sea front and have a drink at The Grove, which has fabulous views across Exmouth's 2 mile (3.2km) long sandy beach both out to sea and across the Exe estuary to the sandspit and nature reserve at Dawlish Warren.

The coastline from Exmouth all the way to Old Harry Rocks on the Isle of Purbeck in Dorset – 95 miles (155km) away – was awarded World Heritage Site status in 2001, the first in England. It's hard to imagine, but the red rocks of this part of east Devon date back 200 million to 250 million years, the Triassic period, when hot desert conditions prevailed. The red colouring comes from the weathering of iron minerals (similar to the Namib Desert in Africa today). The Geoneedle on the red cliffs at

Orcombe Point, just east of Exmouth, marks the inauguration of the World Heritage Site. You can take a boat trip along the coast from Exmouth past Budleigh Salterton's famous pebble beds, deposited by one of the huge rivers that flowed through the desert over 200 million years ago, and today piled up to form a large part of the beach.

the ride

1 From the car park cycle back downhill to the entrance to the park. Turn left on the road and cycle up **Marpool Hill** for about 200yds (183m). Turn left where signed on the cycleway/path (note that cyclists should keep on the left). Follow this tarmac way – watch out for pedestrians – along the top of the park, then between houses, to meet a road.

One of the information boards on the cycle trail

2 Turn right on the pavement up to the traffic lights. Dismount to cross the B3178; turn left, then right after 20yds (18m). Follow this narrow winding tarmac way between fences – take care – to reach another road at **Littleham Cross** (Exmoor Motor Spares, 20yds/18m, left, sells cycle repair kits etc). Cross the road and cycle along Jarvis Close. Keep ahead on a tarmac way, which bears left downhill, then right to reach **Littleham Road**.

3 Cross over. You can push your bike straight ahead on a narrow way between bungalows, or turn right down the road for 100yds (91m), then left into **Bidmead Close**. After 20yds (18m) bear right uphill on a tarmac path – John Hudson Close – to rejoin the old **railway line**.

4 Follow the track under a bridge (Capel Lane – access to the route, and also to the Clinton Arms in Littleham) and on into open countryside. Pass a picnic table on the right with views towards **Dawlish Warren**, and over the 15th-century tower of Littleham's Church of St Margaret and St Andrew, where Lady Nelson is buried. The track becomes gritty and runs pleasantly through farmland, then through **Knowle Hill plantations** (access to Castle Lane). When the line opened in 1903 it was said that it ran through 'beautiful hills and beautiful meadows, with bright colours of earth and field and woodland and gay flowers beside the line'. Sadly it never realised its full potential, and fell to Beeching's axe; the last train ran on 4 March 1967. The cycle route was opened in 1998, and has become a haven for wildlife and flowers.

| 2h00 | 11 MILES | 17.6 KM | LEVEL 1 2 3 |

SHORTER ALTERNATIVE ROUTE

| 1h45 | 10 MILES | 16 KM | LEVEL 1 2 3 |

MAP: OS Explorer 115 Exmouth & Sidmouth

START/FINISH: Phear Park, Exmouth, grid ref: SY 008815

TRAILS/TRACKS: mainly well-surfaced track, short stretches on broad pavements

LANDSCAPE: townscape, woodland and farmland

PUBLIC TOILETS: Phear Park, and just off the route at Littleham Cross (Point 2)

TOURIST INFORMATION: Exmouth, tel 01395 222299

THE PUB: The Grove, Exmouth

 Busy B3178 to pub at Knowle (pavement)

Getting to the start

Exmouth lies east of the mouth of the Exe on the south Devon coast. From the A376 turn left at traffic lights into Gipsy Lane. At the roundabout turn right, then left into Phear Park. From the B3178 Salterton Road turn right. Descend Marpool Hill, bear right at the roundabout, and right into Phear Park.

Why do this cycle ride?

The route follows part of 'The Buzzard', an 80-mile (129km) circular ride through east Devon. It's an easy, quiet ride, mainly along the old Exmouth to Budleigh railway line. There's an optional 1 mile (1.6km) extension at the end for refreshments at the child-friendly Dog and Donkey in Knowle.

Researched and written by: Sue Viccars

CYCLE

5 Pass under another bridge on the top of **Knowle Hill** – the deep cutting here was mainly dug out by hand, with the help of two 'steam navvies' (early steam-driven shovels) – then enjoy a long gentle downhill run under beech trees. Leave the track on a tarmac way that bears right uphill to reach **Bear Lane**, from where there is a glimpse ahead of the wooded top of **High Peak** (515ft/157m) on the coast, site of an Iron Age fort.

6 For a break at the pub, turn right down Bear Lane to the B3178. Turn right downhill (take care – fortunately there is a pavement) to find the Dog and Donkey at the bottom of the hill on the left. To return to **Exmouth**, retrace the route. It is possible to cycle on to **Budleigh Salterton** – named after salt pans that used to be sited at the mouth of the River Otter, the estuary of which is now a nature reserve – but the roads tend to be busy and so this is not recommended for families.

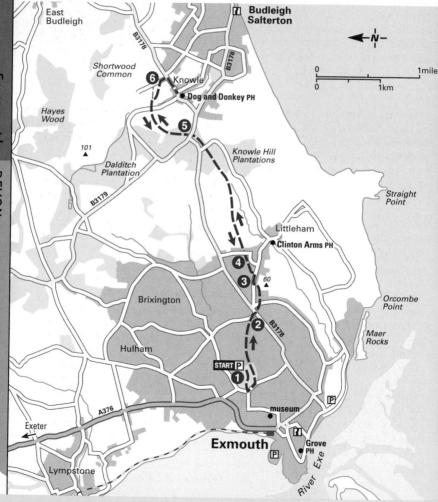

The Grove

A smartly refurbished Young's pub set back from the beach, with a first-floor dining room and balcony enjoying spectacular views across the mouth of the River Exe and along the coast to Torbay. The sheltered rear garden is a super spot for rest and refreshment after time spent on the bike or beach. Inside, the roomy panelled bars are comfortably furnished and feature open fires, well-kept beers, decent wines by the glass, and local prints on the walls.

Food

A menu listing traditional British dishes highlights steak and Young's ale pie, Cumberland sausages and mash, fish pie, beer battered fish and chips, and ham, egg and chips. Lighter meals include ploughman's lunches, Caesar salad and smoked salmon and cream cheese panini.

Family facilities

Children of all ages are welcome inside and there's a family dining area and a children's menu. There's a play area in the garden.

Alternative refreshment stops

Exmouth has an extensive range of pubs and cafés to choose from. There's a café in Phear Park, the Dog and Donkey pub at the suggested turn-around point, or plenty of pubs and cafés in Budleigh Salterton if you choose to cycle on.

☛ Where to go from here

The World of Country Life at Sandy Bay is an all-weather family attraction where kids can meet friendly farm animals, view working models and exhibits from a bygone age, including steam and vintage vehicles, and enjoy a safari train ride through a 40-acre deer park (www.worldofcountrylife.co.uk). For exhilarating rides and huge indoor and outdoor play areas head for Crealy Adventure Park at Clyst St Mary (www.crealy.co.uk). See wholemeal flour being ground at an historic water-powered mill and various pottery, weaving and spinning studios at Otterton Mill (www.ottertonmill.com).

about the pub

The Grove
The Esplanade, Exmouth
Devon EX8 1BJ
Tel 01395 272101
www.youngs.co.uk

DIRECTIONS: from the car park follow signs through the town centre to the Esplanade

PARKING: none – on-street meter parking

OPEN: daily; all day

FOOD: daily; all day

BREWERY/COMPANY: Young's Brewery

REAL ALE: Young's Bitter, Special, Smiles IPA, seasonal beers

Broadhembury

Beech woods and rolling farmland around an unspoilt thatched village.

The Drewe family

Broadhembury is one of those unspoilt showpiece Devon villages that gives you the impression that nothing has changed for centuries and that you've entered a time warp. The picturesque main street is lined with well-preserved cob and thatched

cottages and pretty flower-filled gardens. Much of Broadhembury as you see it today developed as an estate village under the patronage of the Drewe family in the early 17th century, and you get the feeling that this village is not struggling for survival.

St Andrew's Church holds many memorials to members of the family who were highly influential in the development of the village. In 1603 Edward Drewe, Sergeant-at-Law to Queen Elizabeth I, bought Abbey Farm and created The

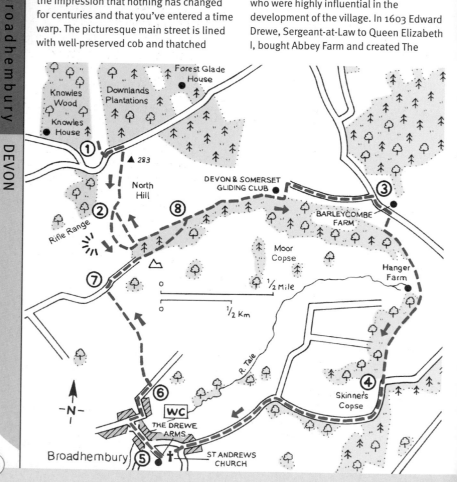

Grange, which remained the family seat for nearly 300 years. Edward Drewe was a successful lawyer, who already owned Sharpham and Killerton. The oak drawing room at The Grange is said to be one of the most beautiful in the country. The house is private, but you can see it from the south east approach road to the village.

The church was consecrated in 1259, but the building dates mainly from the 15th century, constructed of local flint and chalky limestone from Beer. It's set at the end of a cul-de-sac of chestnut trees and has been much restored. The 1480 tower is almost 100ft (30m) high and the timbers of the roof were painted in the late 15th century and were only discovered in 1930 when repair work was carried out. There is also an unusual 15th-century font, which is damaged (probably during the Civil War) and decorated with primitive figures of apostles and clergy, and an 18th-century memorial to Augustus Toplady, who wrote the hymn *Rock of Ages*.

Just a mile (1.6km) to the south east of the village lies Hembury hillfort, on a spur of the Blackdown Hills at 883ft (269m) above sea level. There was a causewayed camp here around 2500 BC, and the site was inhabited until around AD 75.

the walk

1 Return to the road and turn left uphill. Very shortly, just before another 20% sign, a **bridleway sign** points right through a parking area under beech trees. After a few minutes this narrow, level path reaches a signpost and metal gate (left), indicating that you have reached the **Devon and**

Broadhembury DEVON

Somerset Gliding Club. Ignore the gate, continuing on the bridleway.

2 Pass through the next two gates and onto the **airfield**. Turn right along the edge, keeping to the right of the clubhouse. Follow the tarmac drive left over a cattle grid and down the lane to join a road.

3 Turn right; pass **Barleycombe Farm** (on the left), then follow bridleway signs right through a gate, left through another and into a field. Follow the track along the bottom of the field. The path curves right through a stand of beech trees and a metal gate, then runs straight across the next field towards a big beech tree and gate. Take the stony track through the gate. After 100yds (91m) bear right along a grassy path (ignore the gate straight ahead) and through two gates, with a **coniferous plantation** to the right.

what to look for

The Devon and Somerset Gliding Club is near the start of the walk at North Hill, over 900ft (280m) above sea level – a popular spot with skylarks, too. The return leg skirts along the edge of the airfield; the gliders are launched using a steel cable, so it's wise to keep well out of the way. There's something quite magical – and tempting – about watching the gliders drift silently through the air above you, often reaching heights of over 2,000ft (600m).

4 The path ends at a lane; turn right downhill into **Broadhembury**. At **St Andrew's Church** cross the road and go through the churchyard, then under the lychgate and downhill to find **The Drewe Arms** (left) for a welcome break.

5 To continue the walk, from the pub, turn left down the main street to reach the bridge and **ford**. Turn right up the lane, past the playground and up the hill.

6 Just past a group of **thatched cottages** go left over the stile in the hedge and up the field, aiming for a stile in the top left corner. Go over that and straight ahead, keeping the **old farmhouse** and barn conversions to your right. Continue over the next stile, then another, then right, round the edge of the field, and over a small stile ahead into a small copse. Another stile leads into the next field; look straight across to locate the next stile in the beech hedge opposite, which takes you into a green lane.

7 Turn right and walk uphill between conifers, on the left, and fields until a metal gate leads on to another and back on to the **airfield**.

8 Turn left along the edge of the field. Go left over the second gate to rejoin the **bridleway**, which leads back to the road. Turn left downhill to find your car.

Top: The pretty villge of Broadhembury

The Drewe Arms

about the pub

The Drewe Arms
Broadhembury, Honiton
Devon EX14 3NF
Tel 01404 841267

DIRECTIONS:	village is off the A373 north of Honiton; pub is in the village centre
PARKING:	20
OPEN:	closed Sunday evening
FOOD:	daily
BREWERY/COMPANY:	free house
REAL ALE:	Otter Ale, Bitter, Head and Bright
DOGS:	not allowed inside

39

WALK

Broadhembury

DEVON

Set in an archetypal thatched Devon village and dating back to the 15th century, the small, thatched Drewe Arms has a charmingly rustic feel with dado-boarded walls, a pile of magazines next to the inglenook fireplace (with blazing log fire in winter), various rural artefacts and a warm, convivial atmosphere. Striking mullioned windows, carved ceiling beams and quaint old furniture lend the pub its particular tasteful character. The best available West Country produce form the basis of the daily blackboard menus that major in fresh fish. In addition to locally brewed Otter beers there are well chosen house wines, all offered by the glass.

sardines and smoked haddock and Stilton rarebit are all offered in two portion sizes – large and very large. For more dedicated meat-eaters are rare beef and hot chicken baguettes and a Bookmaker's fillet steak with anchovy butter.

Family facilities
Well-behaved children are welcome in the eating area and all dishes can be served as half portions. There is a lawned garden with views of the church for alfresco meals.

Alternative refreshment stops
Café serving tea, coffee and light snacks at Broadhembury Craft Centre.

☞ Where to go from here
At Uffculme (off M5 Junction 27) is the Coldharbour Mill Working Wool Museum (www.coldharbourmill.org.uk). It has been producing textiles since 1790 and is now a working museum, still making knitting wools and fabrics on period machinery. South west of Honiton is Cadhay Manor, a classic Tudor manor. Crealy Adventure Park at Clyst St Mary offers a fun experience for the whole family through rides and indoor and outdoor play areas (www.crealy.co.uk).

Food
Expect on any one day to feast on pollack baked with Cheddar and cream or sea bream with orange and chilli. Steamed mussels with garlic and herbs, griddled

The cliffs of East Devon

WALK

Branscombe DEVON

Along the coast near Branscombe, one of the longest villages in Devon.

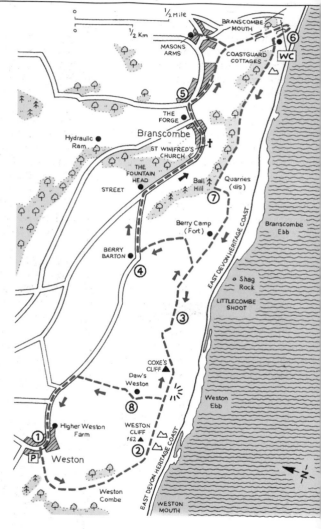

Branscombe

Picturesque Branscombe is one of the most secluded and peaceful villages in this corner of East Devon. Groups of pretty flower-decked cottages sit either side of a long narrow lane that runs gradually down the valley from Street.

This walk takes you to the village along the coast path from Weston. There are extensive views all along the path. The sloping grassy area on the cliff above Littlecombe Shoot is a popular spot for paragliders. At the footpath marker post here a sign leading right appears to direct you straight over the edge of the cliff. This steep, narrow, zig-zag path will take you onto the pebbly beach below.

St Winifred's Church nestles halfway down the valley from Street, and is one of Branscombe's treasures. Dedicated to an obscure Welsh saint, it dates from the 11th century and reveals evidence of continuous development up to the 16th century. The squat tower dates from Norman times and inside are remnants of medieval paintings that once adorned the walls, and an Elizabethan gallery.

Near the village hall, many buildings are owned by the National Trust: the Old Bakery (the last traditional working bakery in Devon until 1987 – now a tea room), Manor Mill (a watermill), and the Forge, complete with working blacksmith.

The beach at Branscombe Mouth gets busy in summer. This is the halfway point of the walk and you can always wander a little way to east or west to escape the crowds.

the walk

1 From the car park take the flinty track over the stile onto the **East Devon Heritage Coast path** signposted 'Weston Mouth'. After 0.5 mile (800m) the sea comes into view at a stile and gate. Go straight on, then veer left across the field to join the coast path at a kissing gate.

2 Go left, steeply uphill (wooden steps) to reach the grassy top of **Weston Cliff**. A kissing gate leads onto Coxe's Cliff and, after a stile, the path runs diagonally away from the coast via a deep combe towards another kissing gate in the top left corner of the field. Cross the next field and through the kissing gate onto grassland above **Littlecombe Shoot**.

3 Go past the **coast path marker** ahead to pass two stands of gorse (left). Turn diagonally left, away from the cliff, towards a banked gap in a scrubby gorse hedge

3h30 — 6.25 MILES — 10 KM — LEVEL 2

MAP: OS Explorer 115 Exeter & Sidmouth
START/FINISH: unsurfaced car park at Weston, grid ref: SY 167890
PATHS: coast path, country lanes, 6 stiles
LANDSCAPE: undulating cliffs, farmland and woodland
PUBLIC TOILETS: behind Branscombe village hall, also in car park at Branscombe Mouth
TOURIST INFORMATION: Seaton, tel 01297 21660
THE PUB: The Masons Arms, Branscombe
❶ This is an undulating walk with two steep ascents and cliff-edge paths. Suitable for older, more experienced children

Getting to the start
Weston is 4 miles (6.4km) east of Sidmouth off the A3052 towards Lyme Regis. Following signs for Weston and Branscombe, pass the Donkey Sanctuary and turn right following signs for Weston. In the centre of Weston, where the road bends sharply left at a little green, turn right into the informal car park.

Researched and written by:
Brian Pearse, Sue Viccars

Aim for a metal gate in the top left corner of the next field, then turn left down the track to join the lane at **Berry Barton**.

4 Turn right down the lane to the **Fountain Head** pub. Turn right again down the valley, passing groups of thatched cottages and **St Winifred's Church** (right). Continue downhill past the post office and the Forge to St Branoc's Well and the **village hall**.

5 Turn right opposite Parkfield Terrace down the lane signposted '**Branscombe Mouth**'. After 200yds (183m) a farm gate leads to a well-signposted path through the field to a footbridge and gate (go left here for **The Masons Arms**). Go through the next meadow and gate. Turn right over a wooden bridge and gate to reach **Branscombe Mouth**.

Previous page: Branscombe's thatched cottages
Below: It's easy to get to the beach from Branscombe

6 Turn immediately right through a kissing gate to join coast path signs uphill beneath the **coastguard cottages** (now a private house). Go through an open gateway and left into the woods via a kissing gate. The path splits here and you can take the cliff top or woodland route. After they rejoin, ignore all paths to the left and right until, after two stiles and 0.5 mile (800m), a signpost points left between grassy hummocks towards the cliffs.

7 Follow the coastal footpath signs to the cliff edge onto **Littlecombe Shoot**. Retrace your steps to Coxe's Cliff, then a stile and kissing gate onto **Weston Cliff**. Turn right into a **wildflower meadow**.

8 Pass the cottage and outbuildings (on the right) through two gateways and onto a track leading to a **tarmac lane**. Go left and in a short while you'll reach **Weston** and your car.

The Masons Arms

Charming 14th-century, thatched and creeper-clad inn, formerly a cider house and well-documented smugglers' haunt. It stands in the centre of picturesque Branscombe, which lies in a steep valley, in National Trust land and only a ten-minute stroll from the sea. Beyond the pretty front terrace is the rustic bar with stone walls, ancient beams, slate floors and an open fireplace, used for spit-roasts on a weekly basis and Sunday lunch. You'll find local Otter ales on handpump, local farm cider and a dozen wines by the glass. The attractive bedrooms are split between the main building and neighbouring terraces of cottages. The walled front terrace is a real sun-trap and very popular in summer.

Food

Popular bar food utilises locally sourced produce, including lobster and crab, and ranges from specials like venison casserole, steak and kidney pudding, local estate steaks, shellfish stew, and oven-roasted sea bass with a black bean sauce, to a tried-and-tested selection of sandwiches, ploughman's lunches and hot filled baguettes. Separate fixed-price menu in the Waterfall Restaurant.

Family facilities

Families are welcome inside the pub and you'll find high chairs for younger family members and smaller portions of adult dishes are readily available.

Alternative refreshment stops

The 14th-century Fountain Head at Street brews its own beer, has great food and a local feel. The National Trust Old Bakery Tearoom can be found near Branscombe village hall and the Sea Shanty café is at the beach at Branscombe Mouth.

☛ Where to go from here

The Donkey Sanctuary (founded in 1969) at Slade House Farm (signposted off the A3052) is a charity that cares for donkeys and is the largest such sanctuary in the world (www.thedonkeysanctuary.org.uk). At the Pecorama Pleasure Gardens in Beer ride on a miniature steam and diesel line and enjoy stunning views across Lyme Bay.

about the pub

The Masons Arms
Branscombe, Seaton
Devon EX12 3DJ
Tel 01297 680300
www.masonsarms.co.uk

DIRECTIONS:	village signposted off the A3052 between Seaton and Sidmouth; pub in village centre close to Point 5 on walk
PARKING:	40
OPEN:	daily; all day
FOOD:	daily
BREWERY/COMPANY:	free house
REAL ALE:	Bass, Otter Ale, Masons Ale, guest beers
DOGS:	allowed in the bar
ROOMS:	22 bedrooms, 20 en suite

Acknowledgements

The Automobile Association would like to thank the following photographers and photo library for their assistance in the prepatation of this book.

Photolibrary.com front cover b.
David Hancock 19, 23, 29, 30, 31, 39, 43, 45t, 47, 48/9, 51, 54, 55, 71, 73, 74, 75, 79, 81, 83, 101, 103t, 103b; Brian Pearce 107, 110, 111, 124/5, 127, 136, 147, 157, 159; Sue Viccars 27, 32/3, 35, 56, 59, 60/1, 63. 64, 67, 88, 91, 93, 95, 97, 99, 115, 117, 119, 120, 121, 123, 140, 141, 143, 153, 155, 163, 164, 167.

The following photographs are held in the Automobile Association's own Photo Library (AA World Travel Library) and were taken by the following photographers.

Peter Baker front cover ccr, cr, 4, 139, 145, 158, 173, 175; E A Bowness 12; Caroline Jones 20, 21, 24/5, 57, 65, 84/5, 87, 104, 105; R Hall 160/1; Andrew Lawson 49, 76, 77, 80/1, 109, 110, 111; Tom Mackie 15; Roger Moss front cover cl, 16, 17, 36, 37, 41, 42, 45b, 96, 161; John O'Carroll 112/3, 128, 129, 131, 132/3, 133, 135, 151; Neil Ray 8/9, 69; Tony Souter front cover ccl, 14b; Rupert Tenison 25; Wyn Voysey 13, 14t, 148, 149, 152, 170, 171. Harry Williams 174.